C000017481

Whoosh. Energetic, refreshing, rich in wisdom and compe[...]
Hooper's book displays a joyous ability to zoom into the h[...]
to connect it to the wider witness of the Bible, and then p[...]
first century context and explore its implications for discipleship and mission with acuity and
compassion, historic and contemporary examples, and his own wide-ranging life experience.
Enjoy.

Mark Greene
Executive Director, The London Institute for Contemporary Christianity

Superb! A Better Way to Live *has encouraged me to 'rest by spirit' in the Psalms and*
Proverbs. Graham Hooper's questions at the end of each section caused me to slow down and
read the passages to savour their rich imagery and absorb their wisdom. For anyone who
wants to move from the kind of information found in self-help management books to having
frameworks for discerning how to navigate business and life decisions, this book is for you.

Wendy Simpson OAM
Chairman, Wengeo Group; Director, World Vision Australia;
Chairman, City to City Australia/Australian Centre for Faith and Work

Full of distilled wisdom, A Better Way to Live *helps us see the good, practical, accessible and*
relevant lessons we can put into practice in our job, community, families, personal lives and
churches. It is grounded in the truth we learn in the Bible and the realities of our ordinary
human lives.

Peter Adam
Vicar Emeritus of St Jude's Carlton, and former Principal of Ridley College

A Better Way to Live *beautifully illuminates how the books of Proverbs and Psalms guide us*
in our choices, relationships, communication, attitudes, ways of being and prayer life. Hooper's
practical reflections on these themes convict and guide us to journey with God in living the life
well lived.

Donna Shepherd
Chair, World Vision International

There are many excellent commentaries on the books of Proverbs and Psalms, but there are
few that reflect seriously on how they can inform and shape our lives. Graham Hooper writes
as a practitioner – one who has lived with these two books and sought to live out their lessons
in the crucible of daily life.

Soo-Inn Tan
Chairman, Graceworks. Singapore

Graham Hooper's excellent book is accessible in style, rigorous in method and highly appealing
in its reflective approach. It presents something for every Christian reader: clergy, scholars and
laypeople alike. The author shows how Proverbs and Psalms, written over 2500 years ago, can
speak into the modern day. By bringing the past into the present, readers are reminded how
they are links in the chain of salvation history, part of God's great narrative.

Peter Riddell
Vice Principal Academic, Melbourne School of Theology

Graham Hooper has written a wise book about Proverbs and Psalms. Biblical wisdom is not only deep, revealing the depths of our hearts and souls, but it is also very practical. As Graham says, the proverbs school our minds, the psalms strengthen our hearts, and both lead us to wise action. This book is full of the richness of Graham's experience as a Christian business executive who regularly speaks and writes on the way our faith relates to the whole of our lives.

Kara Martin
Project Leader, Seed Initiatives, and former Associate Dean, Marketplace Institute

A Better Way to Live *provides a thoughtful and insightful exploration of Psalms and Proverbs for real people seeking to live God's way in the real world. It helps us align our head and heart with God's desires and plans for his people. The message of the book gains greater credibility because its author is someone who has lived all his life in the business world. If you would like to better become God's person in a broken world, this is the book to read.*

John Sweetnam
Principal, Malyon College

Here is a book written from the perspective of the individual in the world of work and business seeking to understand what it means to live out a Christian life. Graham Hooper engages the reader in God's word and gives us the chance to reflect on these truths within the realm of the workplace, where most people spend the majority of their time. This book, with a devotional edge, will help your faith influence your world.

Karl Faase
Chief Executive Officer, Olivetree Media

I loved this book, which takes us on a deeper journey into Proverbs and Psalms and reminds us of the access we have to God's profound wisdom. A Better Way to Live *will reignite your passion for these beautiful and poignant Scriptures.*

Emma Mullings
TV and radio presenter, singer

Don't buy this book if you want a fast read! A Better Way to Live *must be savoured. Graham Hooper takes us on a very practical and spiritual journey into the heart of who we really are and how we should live. Although I have been reading Proverbs and Psalms regularly for over fifty years, I was forced to slow down and embrace a deeper understanding of the true nature of God at work within me.*

Willy Kotiuga
Senior Director of Strategic Studies, Montreal, Canada

A BETTER WAY TO LIVE

52 Studies in Proverbs and Psalms

GRAHAM HOOPER

ACORN PRESS

Published by Acorn Press Ltd, ABN 50 008 549 540

Office and orders:
PO Box 258
Moreland VIC 3058
Australia
Tel/Fax (03) 9383 1266
International Tel/Fax 61 3 9383 1266
Website: www.acornpress.net.au

National Library of Australia Cataloguing-in-Publication entry:
Author: Hooper, Graham, author.
Title: A better way to live: 52 studies in proverbs and psalms / Graham Hooper.
ISBN: 9780994616623 (paperback)
                  9780994616630 (ebook)
Subjects: Bible. Psalms – Criticism, interpretation, etc.
                  Bible. Proverbs – Criticism, interpretation, etc.
                  Christian life – Biblical teaching.
                  Devotional literature.
Dewey Number: 223.706

Cover image: 'Crossroads' by Jacopo Marcovaldi
Source: https://www.flickr.com/photos/bracco/
Licensed under Creative Commons by 2.0 (https://creativecommons.org/licenses/by/2.0/)

Editor: Gina Denholm
Cover design and text layout: Graeme Cogdell, Cogdell Design & Fine Art

For Sue

CONTENTS

Psalms: Songs from the Heart

ACKNOWLEDGEMENTS

I would like to thank Kara Martin and Kris Argall in Australia, and Antony Billington (London Institute for Contemporary Christianity), for reviewing early draft chapters, providing wise advice and encouraging me to press on; and Peter Adam, who read the whole draft manuscript, advised on theological issues and introduced me to Athanasius' wonderful writing on Psalms. Thanks also to those who have kindly provided words of commendation and support for the whole project.

I am particularly grateful to Gina Denholm for her encouraging, insightful and constructive editing, which has made this a much better book than it might otherwise have been.

Looking back, I am thankful to God for all those I have known who have lived out the Christian life, given me a love for the word of God and shown, by their faith in testing times and by the quality of their lives, something of the love and power of Christ. As I write this, it is one week after the passing of Alec Motyer, a much loved and highly respected preacher, writer and Old Testament scholar. I would like to acknowledge with deep gratitude all that Alec taught me during my two years at Trinity College Bristol. I owe him a great deal, and I thank God every time I remember him.

Looking around, I am thankful beyond measure for the continuing love and support of my wife Sue, for all our family, and for our friends in many different parts of the world.

Looking forward, I hope and pray that all who read this book will grow to love the God who inspired these two wonderful books of Proverbs and Psalms.

PREFACE

There is nothing quite so attractive and so powerful as a godly life. I am not thinking here of a few 'super saints'; rather, the many ordinary Christians whose lives show something of the love of Christ, who make a difference for good by the way they live and work. I am thankful to have known many such people, whose lives display a quality that is somehow compelling and who 'make the teaching about God our Saviour attractive' (Titus 2:10).

This is the power of a godly life. Jesus compared the impact that living this way can have on others to the effects of salt and light (Mt 5:13–14). Even a small quantity of salt can arrest the decay of a much larger amount of meat. Even a dim light illuminates a dark room.

In *A Better Way to Live*, I want to point you to two Old Testament books that have been a great inspiration to me: the books of Proverbs and Psalms. They show us the power and love and justice of God, and call for our response.

Together, these books also portray a beautiful picture of a godly life: a way of integrity, love and faithfulness; a way of worship, thankfulness and hope; a better way to live. Better than the bleak emptiness of secular materialism; better than a vague spirituality which has no substance. Better than mere formal religion, because the Christian faith revealed in the Bible, at its core, is not about religious tradition and morality. It is about the reality of the Almighty God who reaches out in grace to lost people. It is about a relationship of faith with Jesus Christ, Lord and Saviour. It is about God calling us to live for him in a world that rejects his authority.

As we learn from God's wisdom in Proverbs and Psalms, so God can transform us and equip us to make a difference for good in this world, like salt and light. It is this conviction that led me to write this book.

INTRODUCTION

We are discussing no small matter, but how we ought to live
(Socrates, *Plato's Republic* 1:352d).

Stand at the crossroads and look; ask for the ancient paths; ask
where the good way is and walk in it and you will find rest for
your souls (Jer 6:16).

Two valuable friends

One of my most treasured possessions, and a constant travelling companion,
is an old, beaten-up paperback copy of the New Testament, with the Old
Testament books of Proverbs and Psalms bound in at the back. I bought
it for a dollar at a second-hand shop. It's A5 in size, so takes up very little
room in my overnight bag, and even fits (at a push) into the back pocket
of my jeans. It's a copy in which I have felt free to scrawl notes, cross-
references and headings to a greater extent than in my hardback Bible at
home.

When I don't have ready access to a whole Bible, hard copy or
electronic, I have come to appreciate this little book. Now, you might want
to argue that the Bible should never be split up in this way, that we need
the whole word of God. Yes indeed! But practicalities of weight and space
for a business traveller mean that compromises have to be made. If you
had to pick only two of the thirty-nine books of the Old Testament to carry
around with you, which ones would you choose? Genesis? Isaiah? Joshua,
Deuteronomy or Ruth, perhaps? As for me, Proverbs and Psalms would be
at the top of my list. Together they show us a better way to live, an authentic
alternative to the secular and materialist life promoted by popular Western
culture. But this alternative is not presented to us as one of a number of
equally good options. Rather, Proverbs and Psalms reveal *God's* way; a
life of faith instead of doubt and fear; a life lived in relationship with God
rather than mere religious observance; a life modelled on the word of God
rather than the standards of the prevailing culture.

The call to be different

The call to be different, in the best possible sense, comes right through the
Bible. The late John Stott chose to underline this truth in his final book,

The Radical Christian, published shortly before his death.[1] He makes the point that 'the first characteristic of the radical disciple is non-conformity'. Stott reminds us that this foundational theme recurs in all four of the main sections of Scripture:

- In the Law: 'You must not do as they do in Egypt, where you used to live, and you must not do as they do in the land of Canaan where I am bringing you. Do not follow their practices. You must obey my laws and be careful to follow my decrees' (Lev 18:3–4).
- In the Prophets: God confronts his people, saying, 'You have not followed my decrees or kept my laws but you have conformed to the standards of the nations around you' (Ezek 11:12).
- In the Gospels: Jesus points to the religious hypocrites and warns his disciples, 'Do not be like them' (Mt 6:8).
- In the New Testament letters: Paul says, 'Do not conform to the pattern of this world, but be transformed by the renewing of your mind' (Rom 12:2).

This call to live differently also runs right through the books of Proverbs and Psalms.

In Proverbs, 'Wisdom calls aloud, she raises her voice in the public square' (Prov 1:20), trying to get our attention, saying in effect, 'You people who mock and who despise knowledge, don't be so stupid. Come and life differently. Live *this* way.' The author contrasts the wise with the simple, who 'love their simple ways' (Prov 1:22) – people without moral direction, without a moral compass.

Similarly, the book of Psalms opens with a very succinct and straightforward description of an authentically godly life:

'Blessed is the one who does not walk in step with the wicked or stand in the way that sinners take or sit in the company of mockers, but whose delight is in the law of the LORD and who meditates on his law day and night' (Ps 1:1–2).

The minister of our local church asked us recently, 'Are you more like a thermometer or a thermostat?' A thermometer simply records the temperature of its environment. A thermostat, on the other hand, gauges the temperature level of its environment, but then makes a difference to its surroundings by adjusting the temperature to the desired level. It sets the temperature, rather than merely adapting to it. In your community and your workplace, do you adapt to the culture or do you help to change it?

---

1   Stott, *Radical Christian*, p. 18.

To ask the same question using the words of Jesus (Mt 5:13–16), are you like salt arresting the decay in society around you, or have you lost your saltiness? Are you like a light, shining in the darkness, or has your light practically gone out?

Different styles, common themes

As we read Proverbs and Psalms, we realise very quickly that these are very different books, in structure, style and content.

In Proverbs we have short sayings, warnings and instructions, and some very apt and humorous word pictures, all grouped into a number of sections.

- Proverbs 1:1–7 explains the purpose of the book.
- Proverbs 1:8—9:18 highlights the value of wisdom.
- Proverbs 10:1—22:16 contains a long series of pithy sayings, entitled 'Proverbs of Solomon'.
- Proverbs 22:17—29:27 is entitled 'Sayings of the Wise'.
- Proverbs 30:1—31:9 contains the 'Wise Sayings of Agur' and the 'Wise Sayings of King Lemuel'.
- Proverbs 31:10–31 closes the book with a description of the 'Wife of Noble Character'.

The topics and style of writing change, sometimes quite abruptly, as we move through the 31 chapters.

Proverbs is not an easy book to read straight through, as we might do with other parts of Scripture such as narratives and letters. It's probably best taken slowly and in small portions, allowing us to think as we read.

Psalms is actually a collation of five 'books' containing songs, poems and prayers grouped around specific themes.

- Book 1: Psalms 1–41
- Book 2: Psalms 42–72
- Book 3: Psalms 73–89
- Book 4: Psalms 90–106
- Book 5: Psalms 107–150.

Why five books? Most probably to match the five books of the Old Testament (the Pentateuch).[2]

Within each of the books, we also find psalms grouped around specific themes. For example, the focus of Psalms 93–100 is on the LORD as the great King. Psalms 113–118 form the *Hallel*, traditionally sung on Passover

---

2   Goldingay comments: 'This correlates to the work of teaching that appears in the Torah ... and the response God looks for in terms of worship and everyday life. Goldingay, *Psalms*, vol. 1, p. 23.

night. Psalms 120–134 are the 'Songs of ascents' for pilgrims and Psalms 146–150 close out the book with songs of praise.

Like Proverbs, we don't necessarily need to read consecutively through the book in order to draw out the meaning of a particular psalm. I suspect most readers focus on one psalm, or just a few verses at a time, turning that into prayer, praise or meditation.

Though Proverbs and Psalms are so different, there are several common themes. From my study of these two wonderful books I have come up with this list. You may well find others.

Common Themes	Examples in Psalms	Examples in Proverbs
The life blessed by God is a godly life*	1	3:13–18
Trusting in God	37:3	3:5–6
Walking the straight path	25:5; 27:1	2:12–15
Understanding God and ourselves	8; 139	9:10
Integrity	25:21	1:4
Foolishness	14:1	9
The guidance of God	25:5	3:5–6
Wise communication	19:14; 141:3	25:11
Learning from God	25:4; 86:11	1:1–7
God our refuge	59:16; 62	4:18; 14:26
Sleeping peacefully at night	3; 4	3:24
Purity of heart	24	4:23; 20:9
Care for the disadvantaged	10:17	15:25
The fear of the LORD	111:10	1:9; 9:10
The sovereignty of God	93; 111	21:1
God's provision	37:25; 111:5	10:3
Generosity	37:26	3:27–28; 31:20

*Note carefully the order. It is the blessing of God that leads to a godly life, not the other way round. In New Testament language, we do not make things right with God through our own efforts, it is through a faith response to his grace. See, for example, Ephesians 2:8–10.

Many authors, One God

King David and King Solomon lived very merry lives;
King David loved his battles and King Solomon loved his wives.

> But when old age came creeping up with many many qualms,
> King Solomon wrote the Proverbs and King David wrote the Psalms
> (Anon).

True? Well ... not quite![3]

Many of the Psalms tell us in their titles who wrote them, and in some cases why. We have 73 Psalms attributed to David, the shepherd boy who became king. Several others were written by Asaph, a temple musician, and some by the Sons of Korah, a guild of temple officials. Still others are attributed to authors such as Solomon (Psalm 72) and Moses (Psalm 90) or are unattributed (e.g., Psalm 1).

The book of Proverbs is traditionally attributed to King Solomon though some scholars see evidence of earlier origin and others have argued that the book in its final form came together after Solomon's time. Chapters 10–22 are attributed directly to Solomon, a king renowned for his wisdom, though later parts of the book refer to contributions from others: Agur (chapter 30), King Lemuel (31:1–9) and a team of scholars in the time of Hezekiah, King of Judah (25:1—29:27).

Beyond authorship, perhaps the bigger mystery is how Solomon, who clearly had an international reputation as a wise leader (1 Kgs 3:5–6) could have made so many foolish mistakes in his later years. As Waltke comments: 'he ceased listening to his own instruction. Spiritual success today does not guarantee spiritual success tomorrow.'[4]

Whoever wrote these two great books, and whenever precisely they were written and collated into their current form, they form part of our inspired Scripture. When we read them with an open, prayerful heart we will find that the God who inspired them will continue to speak through them today.

Learning from Proverbs and Psalms

When I come to study any one of the sixty-six books that make up the Bible, I sometimes ask myself this question: 'What would I learn about God from this book if it were the only book of the Bible I had ever read?' It is a question that helps focus my mind on the message of the particular text I am reading at the time. A different and hypothetical way of asking the same question is, 'What would I lack in my understanding of God if this book were not in the Bible?'

---

3   For more serious and detailed study on structure and authorship the reader may wish to refer to Goldingay, *Psalms*, vol. 1, pp. 25–30; Weiser, *Psalms*, pp. 91–95 and Kidner, *Psalms*, vol. 1, pp. 32–43.

4   Waltke, *Proverbs*, vol. 1, p. 36.

What, then, do we learn about God from Proverbs? We are taught that he loves faithfulness in relationships, honesty in dealing, hard work, care for the poor and generosity. He intends us to use our minds, but in dependence on him, because he is sovereign over all things and we are to make our plans while trusting him for the outcomes. He sets before us two ways to live: the way of wisdom, godliness and integrity on the one hand, and the way of foolishness, unfaithfulness and wasted living on the other. We also learn that we are responsible and accountable for our choices. Like Jesus' parables, Proverbs call us to *think* about our choices in life and their consequences, and to *act* wisely in response. Our choices, and the actions that flow from them, will mould our character and determine our destiny.

What do we learn from Psalms? How impoverished our understanding of God would be if we did not have this book! In Psalms we find that our God is eternal and good, faithful and forgiving, great and awesome, and worthy of our worship and love. We learn from the psalmists, the inspired songwriters and poets, how to live in confidence and faith, and we learn that it is OK to express to God our deepest feelings of doubt and fear.

I find it encouraging that great minds down the centuries have recognised the unique value of this part of the Old Testament. Athanasius, in commending the Psalms to his protégé, Marcellinus, put it like this: 'Son, all the books of the Scripture, both Old Testament and New are inspired by God and useful for instruction [2 Tim 3:16] ... Each of these books you see is like a garden which grows one special kind of fruit: by contrast, the Psalter is a garden which besides its special fruit grows also some of all the rest.'[5]

Psalms is quoted frequently in the New Testament – more than any other Old Testament book, in fact.[6] Many of the psalms speak prophetically about the coming Messiah and have specific fulfilment in Jesus Christ (see, for example, Luke 24:44 and Acts 2:25–28). As we read Psalms, therefore, with the New Testament in our hands, we can expect to learn more about the Saviour, God's own Son, the Lord Jesus Christ.

A perfect balance: the head and the heart

I have come to appreciate the way that the books of Proverbs and Psalms complement each other. If Proverbs is about the head, then Psalms is about the heart. Of course, both books speak to our minds and our hearts, and

---

5 Athanasius, *Letter to Marcinellus.*
6 'In the New Testament, the roughly 54 citations of Psalms exceed those of all other biblical books, with Isaiah's 48 a close second and Deuteronomy's 42, third.' Mowinckel, *Psalms*, p. 20.

both call for response, but I have found this general distinction helpful in reflecting on the ways these two books have functioned in my life.

Proverbs gives us a clear picture of what God's wisdom looks like when acted out in daily life. It takes us to the workplace and the home rather than to a place of worship. It deals, confrontingly, with nitty gritty issues of work, honesty, faithfulness and sex and sets before a picture of the authentic life of faith that fulfils its God-ordained purpose and is not wasted.

Psalms enables us to see inside the hearts of people of faith. We find the writers pouring out their hearts to God in physical danger, in bouts of doubt or depression, in spiritual and emotional crises or in moments of sheer delight. Many of the psalms are intensely personal prayers, while others are rousing songs for communal worship. Wherever we are on the emotional spectrum at any given time, we can find a psalm that echoes our experience. To quote Athanasius again: 'You find depicted in it [Psalms] all the movements of your soul, all its changes, its ups and downs, its failures and recoveries.'[7]

These two books, therefore, seem to me to be in perfect balance. When I go out to face the challenge of my working day, Proverbs shows me the straight path through the maze of difficulties – a clear and sometimes uncompromising approach to life. But I need more than that; I need a song in my heart that comes from knowing God. If Proverbs tells me the right way to live, then Psalms points me to the living God who strengthens me to live it! Proverbs shows us the right path to follow; Psalms motivates us to follow it.

For all their differences, the two books are inextricably linked. What ties them together – indeed, what ties the whole Bible together – is the common theme of a relationship with the unseen, almighty God.

'The fool says in his heart, "There is no God"' (Ps 14:1), but it is the fear of the LORD that is 'the beginning of wisdom' (Prov 9:10).

A practical approach: head, heart … and hands

A Better Way To Live has come out of my own study and reflection of Proverbs and Psalms, and from seeking to apply the truths of these two wonderful books to my own life situations.[8]

My conviction, which underpins this book, is that Proverbs and Psalms together present us with a better way to live – God's way, an approach to life

---

7   Athanasius, *Letter to Marcinellus.*

8   Some of the reflections on Proverbs started life as 'Word of the Week' emails, written by the author and sent out by the London Institute for Contemporary Christianity (www.licc.org.uk) and also posted on http://malyonworkplace.org.au.

in which we see clearly the principles we are to live by, but also one in which we enjoy the forgiving grace of God when we fail and the strengthening power and love of God to press on.

Certainly, we are to understand the truth revealed in Proverbs and Psalms at an intellectual level. But, more important still, God means us to experience the power of that truth and act on it. In that sense, the two books taken together speak to 'the head, the heart and the hands'. Wisdom, like true faith, always results in wise and fruitful actions.[9] This book is for those who want to get to know God better through his word, and to live out their faith by applying this word to everyday life. It is not a commentary, but if it whets your appetite to delve deeper into these two books, then you may like to refer to some of the commentaries, from which I have gratefully drawn, and which are listed in the bibliography.

I have arranged this book into two parts: Proverbs first, and then Psalms. Each part consists of a series of short reflections, grouped in subsections that explore a particular theme found in Proverbs or Psalms, such as understanding, prayer and worship. I have focused on themes rather than attempting consecutive exposition so that the reader, whether alone or in a group study, can dip into it at will. The intentional division into fifty-two chapters allows weekly study throughout a calendar year.

As you work through this book, whether by reading consecutively or by focusing on particular themes and moving back and forth between Proverbs and Psalms, I hope that it will provoke thought and stimulate reflection. If it also then leads you to prayer and worship, a greater love for the God revealed in the Bible and a renewed commitment to living out your faith, then it will be worthwhile.

Try reading a passage from Proverbs and Psalms each day. It will change your life.

---

9   See the letter of James in the New Testament.

PART ONE

PROVERBS:
WISDOM FOR EVERYDAY LIFE

THE PATH OF WISDOM

What do we mean by wisdom? What qualities do you expect to see in a wise person? Someone who thinks wise thoughts and gives us advice when we need it? A person who resolves conflicts rather than causes them? One who does the right thing and makes good life choices? One who is 'doing life well'?

According to the book of Proverbs, wisdom is all of those things and much more. Wisdom begins with knowing God, and in understanding that this is his world and he is in control. We grow wiser insofar as we are ready to listen to and learn from God and from those he has made wise. We grow as we learn to trust in him and put into practice what we learn. Wise thinking leads to wise speaking and wise living. It is a very rare and valuable quality. It is 'more precious than rubies' (Prov 3:15; 8:11). It is also an attractive trait (3:22): wise people are attractive people in the quality of their lives.

1. WISDOM FOR THE EVERYDAY

Read Proverbs 3:13–18

Blessed are those who find wisdom, those who gain understanding
(3:13).

The book of Proverbs is about everyday life. It doesn't tell us much about prayer, worship or the afterlife. It does teach us how to live wisely in this world.

As my favourite commentator on Proverbs, Derek Kidner, says, Proverbs 'seldom takes you to church'. He goes on to explain what he means. 'It calls across to you in the street about some everyday matter … Its function in Scripture is to put godliness into working clothes, to name business and society as spheres in which we are to acquit ourselves with credit to our Lord.'[10]

Wisdom at work

Proverbs is a great book to turn to before starting work in the morning. Why? Because it deals directly, through pithy and sometimes funny illustrations, with many of the issues we face in our working day: honesty, the value of hard work, dealing with conflict and willingness to listen and learn. It warns us about the folly of self-promotion, unfaithfulness and deceit. It helps us understand what foolishness and wisdom look like in the real world and how faith in God works out in day-to-day plans and actions.

We need wisdom for work, because we spend most of our waking hours focused on work. By 'work' I mean everything we do that requires effort, whether study, routine chores at home, raising children, voluntary work, paid work, looking for employment or running a business. Our daily tasks may not require us to make weighty or critical decisions every day, but they do require us to speak, act and react in seemingly mundane situations. As we make hundreds of small decisions, affecting others and influencing the direction of our own lives, we have the Holy Spirit as our guide and the Bible as our teacher. Both point us to wisdom as a precious gift that we should highly prize.

I have spent most of my life working in the infrastructure business, a job that has taken me to some twenty countries. My wife and I have lived for extended periods in Africa, Asia, Europe and Australia. Whatever the

10 Kidner, *Proverbs*, p. 33.

work situation, and whatever culture we are in, the book of Proverbs speaks to us about how to deal with difficult situations and difficult relationships. It teaches, warns, encourages and inspires. It is a very practical book and deals with 'real world' problems, but it is also a very spiritual book, because God speaks to us through it.

Learning from mistakes and failures

Proverbs contains many warnings, most of which could be summed up in the phrase, 'Don't mess up your life by foolish words and foolish actions.' Our TV news bulletins and social media feeds serve up a daily diet of stories about people behaving badly. Even as I write, the lead news story in front of me describes politicians and developers caught up in corruption scandals that are gradually being uncovered in a commission of inquiry, a process that is already damaging lives, relationships and reputations irreparably. The same front page also reports on a highly regarded, supposedly intelligent, sports celebrity caught sniffing cocaine in a public toilet. Let's look and listen and learn!

In our own spheres of work we may encounter bullies, cheats and gossips – people who mess up their own lives and spoil those of others. In my work, I have seen people caught up unnecessarily in conflict, and sometime lawsuits, because of things that they have unwisely said, written, emailed, tweeted or posted on the internet.

I know the damage I can cause by unwise words and actions, saying or doing the wrong thing at the wrong time. In that fanciful – but, I think, delightful – film *Groundhog Day* (Columbia Pictures, 1993), the main character, played by Bill Murray, is repeatedly given the opportunity to relive his daily encounters. Each time, he handles the situations better as he learns from his mistakes and acts and speaks more wisely. There are times when we might wish for our own 'groundhog day', an opportune re-run of the situations in which we messed up.

In real life we don't get to relive our mistakes, but we do have the opportunity to learn from them and grow wiser from the experience. If we are wise, we learn from the mistakes of others and from our own. To listen to God's warnings in Proverbs is even wiser.

Benefits and blessings

But Proverbs is much more than instructions and warnings. It is a very positive book. It celebrates the benefits and blessings that come to the one who chooses to live wisely.

Wisdom will bring long life and prosperity (3:2). It will preserve our reputations and good names (3:4). The wise ones are well respected and well reputed. They trust in the Sovereign LORD (3:5, 6). They are humble, not wise in their own eyes (3:7–8). Their generosity towards God will bring them prosperity (3:9–10). They are willing to take correction from others (3:11–12).

Proverbs also inspires us with role models of wise people. It pictures wisdom as a quality that enhances our lives and relationships. When people speak and act wisely at work, then work becomes a more enjoyable experience. So it is in every part of life. Wisdom in action actually beautifies our lives and transforms relationships.

I am very thankful to have known some very wise people and to have learned from them. When I first became a Christian while living in East Africa in my twenties, there were many things in my life that were clearly inconsistent with Christian faith. Looking back, I am grateful for the practical wisdom of those Christian leaders who encouraged me in my new faith instead of pointing out all my shortcomings. Their wisdom helped change my life. They also left me an example of wise leadership to follow. Later, while working in Mauritius, I met Bert, an electrician whose example of living as a Christian in a secular workplace is indelibly printed on my memory. He would react to some of my questions and wild statements about moral issues and ethical standards at work with just a smile and a raised eyebrow, rather than giving me a lecture. That silence spoke more clearly than any words.

Whoever finds and exercises wisdom is truly blessed (3:18).

Reflection

1. Why is wisdom such a rare quality?
2. According to Proverbs 3:13–16, why is the one who finds wisdom so 'blessed'?
3. In what areas of your life do you need wisdom right now?

2. PRAGMATISM, OR SOMETHING MORE?

Read Proverbs 1:1–9

For gaining wisdom and instruction; for understanding words of
insight; for receiving instruction in prudent behaviour, doing what
is right and just and fair; for giving prudence to those who are
simple, knowledge and discretion to the young – let the wise listen
and add to their learning, and let the discerning get guidance –
for understanding proverbs and parables, the sayings and riddles
of the wise (1:2–6).

Why was Proverbs written? It is always helpful when a book of the Bible
explains its purpose clearly. It saves us from the mistakes we may make
when we try to impose our own ideas retrospectively. The author sets
out his intent clearly in the opening verses: learn wisdom, and put it into
practice!

According to Proverbs, wisdom has many facets. It consists of:
- Instruction: the process of disciplined learning
- Understanding or insight: the ability to assess people and situations
- Prudence or wise dealing: knowing the right thing to do at the right
  time
- Discretion: the ability to know how to handle people, situations and
  information entrusted to us
- Knowledge: not just intellectual ability, but knowledge of God
  himself (2:5; 3:6).

Doing the right thing

At this point it all sounds rather unexciting. Is this just a boring book of
practical instructions, an ancient version of the self-help books and glossy
magazine articles we find in the airport bookstore? Or is it like one of
those dreaded lectures from a teacher, a parent or a boss, telling us how we
should behave, which only leaves us feeling bad?

Perhaps it is just a useful tool to help us succeed in life. Take away the
references to the LORD and we may be left with a book that tells us how to
succeed in our work and relationships.

But this raises the question: Do we only speak and act wisely because it
helps us get along and succeed? The child who decides to comply with their
parents' instruction to tidy up a messy room, because this will ensure the

promised treat later on, understands this sort of pragmatism very well. So does the business owner who decides not to cheat her customers because she knows honesty will build trust and lead to repeat business and higher profits. So does the bank executive who announces his bank's intention to clean up corruption in his organisation with the comment, 'Becoming ethically strong will give us a competitive edge.' Is that all that is being advocated here: 'Do the right thing because I will get an advantage by doing so'?

Are we to speak and act in a certain way because it is the right thing? And, if so, who says it is the right thing?

In response to the first question: it is true that there is often a strong alignment between what is right and what is to our advantage. But Proverbs challenges us to do the right thing even when it does *not* bring us any personal benefit. In response to the second question: although Proverbs contains no 'Thus says the LORD' statements, the right path is defined by what is consistent with the character of the LORD, not, as in Western culture today, by what popular opinion decrees.

The wisdom of God

Proverbs goes far beyond good advice. It reveals a true wisdom, one that is not to be confused with our educational qualifications, our IQ levels, or with being street smart or business savvy. It reveals that such wisdom stems from the recognition that there is a God who made us, to whom we are accountable. The key statement at the end of the prologue sets all that follows in the context of something much bigger: 'The fear of the LORD is the beginning of knowledge, but fools despise wisdom and instruction' (1:9).

This is a book about faith and our relationship to God, Qualities like generosity, integrity, and faithfulness are presented as much more than just desirable attributes that improve relationships; they are facets of the character of God. The wisdom of God is much more than pragmatism.

Wisdom and godliness go together. Truly wise people are good people. Indeed, they are *godly* people. This underpins the whole of the book of Proverbs.

Reflection

1. Consider each of the facets of wisdom presented in Proverbs 1:1–9. In what areas of your daily life do you need to acquire and apply
   - instruction?
   - understanding?

- prudence?
- discretion?
- knowledge?
2. Think of someone you regard as truly wise. How are these aspects of wisdom displayed in their life?
3. How would you explain the difference between 'common sense' and the wisdom we find in Proverbs?

3. WISDOM AND FAITH

Read Proverbs 3:5–8

Trust in the LORD with all your heart and lean not on your own
understanding; in all your ways submit to him, and he will make
your paths straight (3:5–6).

Differentiating Proverbs from any other book of wise sayings or quotations,
and elevating it way above the level of moral platitudes, is the statement in
the first chapter that 'the fear of the LORD is the beginning of knowledge'
(1:7). The phrase occurs again in chapter 9 with slightly different wording
which links wisdom, knowledge and understanding together in the
context of our relationship to God: 'The fear of the LORD is the beginning
of wisdom, and knowledge of the Holy One is understanding' (9:10). We
are encouraged to put our trust in him, submit to his authority and look to
him for direction.

Trust in the LORD

Notice the use of the word 'LORD', which occurs more than one hundred
times in Proverbs.[11] It is God's covenant name, Yahweh, the name he
revealed to Moses (Exod 6:3). Notice also the implicit assumption here
that God exists, and that it is possible to know him – not just to know about
him – because he has revealed himself to us and he speaks to us through
his word. Therefore, 'understanding' is not merely intellectual capacity
developed through natural ability and education; understanding requires
a personal relationship with God. Notice also the implicit assumption that
God cares about us, our work, our relationships and, most of all, about our
relationship with him.

This, then, is a book about faith, to help and encourage us. It is for
people of faith: people who believe in God, who have to come to know
God and who want to live a life consistent with the character of God. So
the book exhorts us to 'Trust in the LORD with all your heart' and not to
rely on our own understanding. This means that we are to order our whole
lives under God, and not just to go to him for help when we run out of
ideas! We are to acknowledge and submit to his rule over our lives 'in all

---

11 As distinct from 'Lord' (*adonai*), which is commonly used in English Bibles as the translation of the
Hebrew word for 'sovereign'.

our ways' (3:6). This means seeking God's guidance in all our decisions about the way we use our time and spend our money, and relying on God's help and strength in the work we do, the way we do it and the way we treat people. As we recognise his control over all our lives, relationships and future plans, we have his promise that he will then 'direct our paths' (3:6) and show us the way forward.

So, all that is written in Proverbs is to be read and understood within the overarching worldview that the sovereign LORD, the covenant God, is in charge. This is God's world. We are accountable to him, and true wisdom is found in that knowledge and in a relationship with him.

Planning and trusting

But how do we balance the need to *plan* with the need to *trust*? How do faith and wisdom work together? When do we need to wait passively for God to intervene and when do we need to be proactive? When do we trust God to work things out and when do we need to act? When and how are we to rely on our own skills, experience and knowledge, and when are we to rely on the LORD?

The answer of Proverbs seems to be that these are the wrong questions. It is not either/or. It is both/and. For example, we pray: 'Give us this day our daily bread.' We ask God for food, but do we expect it to arrive miraculously at our door? No! We go out to work, earn our money and spend it at the shop. We bring home our groceries, cook our food, sit round the dinner table and then (rightly) thank God for providing for us.

When we pray for a job, we don't just lie back on the sofa 'praying it in'; we 'get out there', submit our resumes, make a few calls and pray that God will work out his purpose. We do not always receive clear guidance about our every move. We pray, we plan and we trust in the sovereignty of God. Sometimes God does provide for us in a surprising way, sometimes he guides us very clearly, but often he calls us to plan *and* to trust him. We are to trust in him before we act, as we act and after we have acted.

Trust in the LORD is to underpin our whole lives and to permeate all our thinking and doing. We are to use our God-given skills and knowledge wisely. We are to plan wisely. But we are also to commit all our plans to the sovereign LORD and trust him to fulfil his perfect will. Wise planning and faith are complementary and tightly interwoven, not mutually exclusive. Both are an expression of God-given wisdom.

So as we make our plans prayerfully, using all the knowledge, wisdom and experience God has given us, we have the gracious promise: 'Commit to the LORD whatever you do, and he will establish your plans' (16:3). But we are also warned, 'Do not boast about tomorrow, for you do not know what a day may bring' (27:1), and reminded, 'In their hearts humans plan their course, but the LORD establishes their steps' (16:9).

It is the LORD who is in control.

Reflection

1. 'The fear of the LORD is the beginning of knowledge' (1:7). Why is this so? See also Proverbs 9:10.
2. According to Proverbs, wise living combines trust in God in every area of life with practical planning, hard work and accountable decision-making. How do you balance the need to plan with the need to trust God?
3. In what ways do you need to trust God more?

4. THE VALUE OF WISDOM

Read Proverbs 8:1–21

Choose my instruction instead of silver, knowledge rather than
choice gold, for wisdom is more precious than rubies, and nothing
you desire can compare with her (8:10–11).

Wisdom is a greatly undervalued quality in our society. It is not on most people's wish lists.

We value skill, experience, reliability and commitment. We reward creativity, sporting prowess and academic achievement. But wisdom seldom rates a mention. We prize physical health, nutritious food and exercise. We recognise the importance of getting an education, preparing our children for a career and playing a useful role in society. But we hear very little about wisdom and the importance of growing in wisdom. We give great respect to celebrities, the rich, the attractive, the clever and the athletic, but not to the wise.

Think back to any job interview you have attended. Was wisdom one of the assessment criteria? Probably not. And yet, Proverbs tells us that wisdom is more valuable than silver, gold or precious jewels, and absolutely essential for us in order to steer our way through all the challenges and temptations of life.

More precious than rubies

Wisdom is so valuable because it brings knowledge of God. As we have seen, wisdom encompasses understanding, discipline, prudence, knowledge and discretion (1:2–3). These may sound to us like common sense, but true wisdom is very uncommon: 'She is more precious than rubies' (3:15). Men and women can succeed in life, rise to the top of their profession, and still not have true wisdom, because 'the fear of the LORD is the beginning of wisdom' (9:10). Without knowing God, you cannot discover the meaning or purpose of your life, and therefore you cannot be truly wise.

Wisdom is also valuable because wise people transform homes and workplaces by the way they speak and act, by the way they handle conflict. They make a difference for good by their honesty, hard work, faithfulness and reliability, and by their thoughtful insight and generosity of spirit. Such people also bring with them a depth and maturity that comes from a faith that is integrated with the whole of life, and an attitude which sees daily work as an essential part of worship of God.

Proverbs surely has much of great value to teach us in the twenty-first century about behaviour, relationships and work. Indeed, if we all made Proverbs our regular reading we might be able to dispense immediately with many of the thousands of self-help books and personal development programs that promise the secrets of success in life!

The effects of wisdom go much deeper than material prosperity: 'My fruit is better than fine gold; what I yield surpasses choice silver' (8:19).

Learning about value

Wisdom is precious, because through wisdom we learn what is of real and lasting value in this life. I have learned, often through my own mistakes and foolishness, what I really value. Sometimes we get things out of proportion. We get so wrapped up in ourselves that we value money, success, recognition and possessions more than relationships, and more than the love and wisdom of God. Sometimes life teaches us hard lessons. We may only realise how much we value our marriage, our family or friendships when we are in danger of losing them. It may take a crisis to remind us how much we need God and what a great privilege it is to bring our prayers to him.

The daughter of a friend of mine was badly injured in a car crash. Her father had only recently bought her the car, which was now a write-off. Said my friend, 'As I sat by her bedside, praying to God for her recovery, I never gave the car a thought.' Of course! *Things* don't give meaning to life; it is *relationships* that are more precious than possessions. To have learned that lesson is to have grown in wisdom.

The world doesn't value wisdom very highly, but Scripture tells us clearly that time and energy spent in seeking wisdom will yield better returns than any monetary investment. 'For [wisdom] is more profitable than silver and yields better returns than gold' (3:14).

If you are learning to value wisdom, then you are wise indeed. If you know someone who is truly wise, you know you have met someone special.

Reflection

1. Think of some of the terms we commonly use to describe people: smart, savvy, emotionally intelligent, practical. How does wisdom differ?
2. Does wisdom necessarily include any of these characteristics?
3. In what ways have you learned to value wisdom in your life?

5. RECOGNISING WISDOM

Read Proverbs 13:1–16

All who are prudent act with knowledge, but fools expose their
folly (13:16).

What do we expect to see in a person who is truly wise? Proverbs tells us
that wisdom is much more than a cerebral quality. We recognise wisdom
in people's thinking, in their words, in their actions and in their attitudes.
Wisdom permeates the whole of life.

Thought, word and deed

Wise people listen to advice (13:1, 13) and are willing to be corrected
(13:18). They know the right time to speak and the right time to say silent.
When they do open their mouths, what they say is worth listening to.

A member of our church home group has a wonderful ability to
articulate – directly, clearly and in just a few words – the thoughts that the
rest of the group is struggling to express. When she speaks, we all listen.

Wisdom also involves wise thinking: the ability to weigh up what to
say and do in difficult situations and to discern the true motives of others.
Exercising this sort of wisdom keeps us from saying and doing stupid
things and causing conflict unnecessarily: 'Discretion will protect you, and
understanding will guard you' (2:11).

True wisdom is seen not just in wise words and wise thinking, but also
in prudent actions: 'All who are prudent act with knowledge, but fools
expose their folly' (13:16). Proverbs has much to say about such practical
godliness: about fair dealing in business; about righteousness, integrity and
kindness to the poor; about avoiding sexual temptation; about the virtue of
hard work. Prudence is not just 'doing the right thing', but doing the right
thing *at the right time.*

Reaching elsewhere into Scripture, we find that the wise person also has
the right attitude to life. They recognise how short life is and set priorities
in the light of that. Their prayer each day is: 'Teach us to number our days,
that we may gain a heart of wisdom' (Ps 90:12). If we are wise, we will ask
God for help to make the most of the opportunites open to us, rather than
wasting the precious days he has given us. This principle is echoed in New
Testament teaching about the qualities of a life controlled by the Holy Spirit:
'Be very careful then, how you live – not as unwise but as wise, making the

most of every opportunity, because the days are evil' (Eph 5:15).

Wisdom is seen in wise leadership. King Solomon, when still a young man and very conscious of the huge responsibility entrusted to him, prayed, 'So give your servant a discerning heart to govern your people and to distinguish between right and wrong' (1 Kgs 3:9). If you hold any position of leadership at work or in the community, or carry any responsibility at home, you might have prayed a prayer like this: 'Lord, give me wisdom. Show me the right thing to do.'

As we live out our faith in this complex world, which confronts us with so many difficult choices, we are wise if we allow the word of God to guide and teach us, to influence our thinking and transform our behaviour (Rom 12:1–2).

The wisdom of Jesus

If we want the best example of wisdom in all its facets, we can look to Jesus Christ. During his earthly ministry, his words were full of truth and power.[12] They showed deep understanding of the people he encountered. He always spoke the right words at the right moment and did the right thing at the right time.

The Gospels record for us many examples of the wisdom of Jesus. There was the time when the Jewish leaders brought to him a woman who had been caught in the act of adultery, which, according to the strict letter of their law, deserved death by stoning. Trying to trap him, they asked Jesus what should be done with her. After a few moments' silence, Jesus spoke these famous words: 'Let any one of you who is without sin be the first to throw a stone at her' (Jn 8:7). The tension was diffused. The woman was safe. The people started to drift away. John notes that the older ones left first; perhaps they were more aware of their own failings than were the young.

On another occasion, some Pharisees asked Jesus, 'Is it right to pay the imperial tax to Caesar or not?' (Mt 22:17). This was another clever attempt to trap Jesus. If he said no, then they could go to the Roman authorities and have him charged with inciting rebellion. If he said yes, he would lose the support of the common people, who hated the Roman occupation of their land.

Jesus invited the Pharisees to show him a coin, and asked whose image was on it. The emperor's head was on the coin. Then came Jesus' words of wisdom: 'Give back to Caesar what is Caesar's, and to God what is God's'

---

12 See, for example, Jn 6:68.

(22:21). Matthew adds this comment: 'When they heard this, they were amazed. So they left him and went away' (22:22).

Take a moment to reflect on this wisdom of Jesus, which left his critics speechless and amazed. He answered their question, which they must have spent some time preparing, with the barest minimum of words. In so doing, he laid down a profoundly wise and timeless principle about how we are to live out our faith in God as good citizens, accountable to the governing authorities.

It was said of Jesus that, as a child, he 'grew and became strong; he was filled with wisdom' (Lk 2:40).

Let us learn from him.

Reflection

1. As we read the Gospels, on what occasions (other than the two referred to above) do we see Jesus' perfect wisdom in his words and in his actions?

2. Think of some specific situations where someone's wisdom, shown in timely advice or practical action, has had an impact on your life.

6. HOW CAN I GET WISDOM?

Read Proverbs 2:1–6

For the LORD gives wisdom; from his mouth come knowledge and understanding (2:6).

How do we become wiser people? In the language of Proverbs, how can we get wisdom? The answer has a number of strands.

Revelation

First, wisdom comes by revelation. It comes from God: 'the LORD gives wisdom'. That is why we are invited to read and study and apply the revealed word of God to our lives.

Proverbs is a good place to start; it is not, of course, the only place in the Bible that teaches us about wisdom. Wisdom is part of the character of God, and so we see God's wisdom revealed right through the Scriptures in all he says and does. It is there throughout the Old Testament – in the Law, the Prophets and the Writings – but it is given particular attention in the books commonly referred to as 'wisdom literature': Psalms, Proverbs, Job, Ecclesiastes and the Song of Solomon, which are part of the Writings.

In the New Testament we see the wisdom of Jesus in action in the Gospels, in the penetrating wisdom of his words, the ways in which his actions are perfectly fitted to the situation and in his whole way of living under the authority of his Father (Jn 6:38) and the Scriptures (Mt 4:4, 7, 10).

The New Testament letters also teach us about wise living. Paul reminds us that the cross of Christ is at the centre of God's wisdom as the only way of salvation for lost people, even though it appears as foolishness to non-believers (1 Cor 1:21). The letter of James deals with many of the themes of Proverbs, such as wise speech, consistent behaviour and practical concern for the poor.

But it is the book of Proverbs that deals most particularly with the topic of wisdom. It is surely God's special gift, given to help us to think, speak and act wisely.

Asking God

Second, we gain wisdom by asking God for it. 'If any of you lacks wisdom, you should ask God, who gives generously to all without finding fault, and it will be given to you' (Jas 1:5).

To ask means that first we must recognise our need. Those who of us who have been brought up to be self-reliant and proud of our abilities find even this act of asking God for wisdom to be humbling. As Kidner expresses it, wisdom is 'not for the man "wise in his own eyes": he thinks he has arrived and indeed he has, for he will never get a step further.'[13]

There is a paradox here. If we think we are wise enough that we do not need to ask God to make us wiser, then we are not wise at all.

Commitment

Third, wisdom comes by discipleship. Learning from God and living for God requires a committed approach. The verbs in the opening verses of Proverbs 2 show the active nature of learning wisdom: 'If you *accept* my words and *store up* my commands within you, *turning* your ear to wisdom and *applying* your heart to understanding – indeed if you *call out* for insight and *cry aloud* for understanding, and if you *look* for it as for silver and *search* for it as for hidden treasure, then you will understand the fear of the LORD and find the knowledge of God' (2:1–4, italics mine).

This is not a casual sort of faith; rather, it is a picture of seeking God and his wisdom with our whole hearts. As we read the Bible we need to study it, accept it, store it up in our hearts and minds, give it our best attention and put it into practice. More, if we are wise, and if we want to become wiser, we will cry out to God from deep within our being for more of this precious gift.

Seeking wisdom is like seeking treasure. As Jesus said, 'Where your treasure is, there your heart will be also' (Mt 6:21). What we value most shows what is dearest to our hearts, and what is dearest to our hearts is where we direct our energies and efforts.

Ask yourself, 'Where in my list of priorities is knowing God better and finding his wisdom? Do I need to re-order my priorities?' God has promised that if we seek, we will find: 'You will seek me and find me when you seek me with all your heart' (Jer 29:13).

Reflection

Step outside Proverbs for a moment and read 1 Corinthians 1:18–25.

1. How is the wisdom of God demonstrated in the death of Jesus Christ on the cross?

2. Why does that seem to be such foolishness to the non-believer (1 Cor 1:18)?

---

13 Kidner, *Proverbs*, p. 36.

3. What does Paul mean by the 'wisdom of the world' (1 Cor 1:20) and why can't it lead to knowledge of God? Refer also to Proverbs 9:10.

7. THE GUARDING POWER OF WISDOM

Read Proverbs 2:6–22

[The LORD] is a shield to those whose way of life is blameless,
for he guards the course of the just and protects the way of his
faithful ones (2:7–8).

Chapter two of Proverbs is introduced rather dryly in my Bible under the heading, 'Moral Benefits of Wisdom.' The text itself explains its message more simply and directly: 'Wisdom will save you from the ways of wicked men' (2:12).

Keeping out of trouble

I have a friend who was brought up in a Christian home. He grew up as a believer and enjoyed a strong, happy marriage and a fulfilling life. One day he confided in me that he sometimes wished he had a more dramatic testimony. He thought his life might have a much greater impact on others if he had led a drug-ridden, wildly debauched life before turning to Christ so that he could tell others how God had saved him! My friend felt that his life had been too boring and was not enough of a testimony to God's saving power.

But then, as he reflected on some Scriptures like this passage in Proverbs, he began to realise how much God had saved him *from* already. He had saved him from many of the major temptations offered to the young in this world. He had saved him from messing up his life with stupid decisions in his adolescent years. He had saved him from the misery of broken, faithless relationships. He had saved him from corruption in business, and from the drink and drug problems that had led some of his peers to jail. This, according to Proverbs, is the power of wisdom, and this is clearly one of the main uses to which we are to put this book of Proverbs – to keep us from stupid behaviour and from following evil people.

Wisdom is far more than understanding; it saves us from much avoidable trouble. This theme is repeated several times so that we get the message:

- 'Discretion will protect you, and understanding will guard you' (2:11). Wisdom is like a personal security guard, keeping us away from temptation.

- 'Wisdom will save you from the ways of wicked men' (2:12). We are not going to go through life unscathed by the evils of the world we live in, but the principle here is that if we think, speak and act wisely, we don't invite trouble unnecessarily.
- 'Wisdom will save you also from the adulterous woman' (2:16). In our society, sexual temptation can be overwhelming. Wisdom is God's gift to us to keep us from destroying relationships and ruining our lives through acting first and thinking second.

I once heard Billy Graham say that he read through Proverbs every month. It was a way of keeping his feet firmly on the ground as he faced the many temptations thrown at him while travelling away from home, speaking to large crowds, dealing with money donated to his evangelistic work and meeting regularly with the rich and powerful.

Dealing with temptation

Jesus taught his disciples to pray to God the Father that he would not 'lead us into temptation'. As we begin our daily work, whether in an outside workplace, in the home or in our own business, we face temptations to behave in ways we know are contrary to the will of God as clearly expressed in the Bible. We may be tempted to be dishonest, cheat on our expenses, avoid taxation by backdoor cash deals or short-change our customers. We may be tempted to compromise our professional ethics, substitute lower-quality materials than specified in our products, take safety shortcuts or mistreat the children under our care. We may be tempted to abuse our power to get what we want or undermine the authority over us, causing unnecessary hurt in the process. And that's just before lunchtime!

As we go out into the world, with all its godless pressures, we are called to put on 'the full armour of God' (Eph 6:11), including 'the sword of the Spirit, which is the word of God' (Eph 6:17). The book of Proverbs is a very useful part of that armour. Why? Because it deals openly with the practical temptations of money, sex and power (and many others) that we face. It shows us the foolishness of ignoring wise advice, and the need to grow in wisdom as part of arming ourselves for the battle.

Perhaps, like me, you have struggled with temptations of various kinds. You may have said things to people that you wish you hadn't, and done things you regret. There may have been times when you wish you had spoken out rather than kept silent, or at least expressed yourself more clearly. There may be conflict situations that you would have liked to resolve better.

But this isn't a book about regrets over our past failures. Proverbs is part of the whole Bible, which brings us good news and tells us how God has reached out in love to fallible and unloving people like us. He sent his Son Jesus Christ into this world to save, transform and renew. We can begin each day with a clean slate of sins forgiven, with the presence of God and with the Spirit of God in our lives. We also go out with his word, the Bible, given 'to make you wise for salvation through Christ Jesus' (2 Tim 3:15).

Good friends will always look out for us, advising and cautioning us because they don't want to see us mess up. Loving parents will teach and warn and encourage their children, equipping them with the knowledge and wisdom needed to keep them out of trouble and make the best of the opportunities open to them as they grow up and move out into the world. God is our most faithful friend and our loving Father, and as we read Proverbs his love and care shine through. He knows where we are most vulnerable to temptation, and he reveals to us his wisdom, equipping us to deal with temptation and to make wise choices that will keep us on the right path.

'Wisdom will save you from the ways of wicked men' (Prov 2:12). If we are wise, we make God's wisdom our daily study.

Reflection

1. What are the big temptations you most commonly face? How do you deal with them?
2. What means does God use to help us face and overcome temptation? See 1 Corinthians 10:13; Hebrews 2:18, 4:15–16.
3. Let us pause to thank God for his protection and guidance in our lives (see Prov 2:7–8) and for his promise and gift of forgiveness and a new start when we fail (1 Jn 1:8–9).

RIGHT CHOICES

As we think about how wisdom is applied day to day, we find that Proverbs presents the options to us in a series of stark contrasts.

Will we choose to be lazy or to work hard: the way of dishonesty or the way of integrity? Will we be generous with all that God has blessed us with, or abuse our privileged position and exploit others for our own gain? Are we narcissistic, self-promoting people, or are we humble? Are we foolish, or are we wise? To help us understand what wisdom looks like, Proverbs goes to some lengths to reveal to us the essence of foolishness and the actions and lifestyle that result from foolish choices.

I recently attended a seventieth birthday party. As part of the formalities, the man's thirty-five-year-old son gave a short speech in honour of his much-loved father. He said this (which I have his permission to quote!): 'Dad is a man who has chosen the path of hard work, sacrifice, honesty and compassion over the alternatives of laziness, selfishness, rudeness, drunkenness and hard-heartedness that can sometimes overcome the male identity.'

If the original writers of Proverbs could have been present to hear these words, they might have stood up and applauded! Here was a Christian man who had come through many difficult situations, but who, by God's grace, had clearly made the right choices and left a great example for his son in the process.

8. WISDOM, NOT FOOLISHNESS

Read Proverbs 9:1–18

Leave your simple ways and you will live; walk in the way of
insight (9:6)

In Proverbs, wisdom is contrasted with foolishness, the wise person is
contrasted with the fool, and the outcomes of both wise and foolish choices
are described in word pictures so that we get the message. As we read, we
face the question: which path will we choose?

Three kinds of fool

There are different kinds of foolishness. Three Hebrew words are commonly
translated 'fool' in our English Bibles, and each gives us a different angle
on the problem..[14]

Kesil, the most common of the three terms, occurs fifty times. It implies
dullness and obstinacy, but the root of the trouble is spiritual. This sort of
fool keeps coming back to make the same mistake over and over, 'like a
dog that returns to his vomit' (26:11). They love to speak first and think
second, and enjoy impressing opinions on others (18:6–7). The slogan
'always certain, seldom right' would fit this person well.

Ewil occurs nineteen times. Its use is very similar to *kesil*, but it has
a darker meaning. This sort of fool is quarrelsome. They lack restraint
and a sense of proportion (27:3, 29:9). They are certainly not interested in
listening to advice.

Nabal occurs three times in Proverbs. It indicates a closed mind. This
sort of fool is stubborn or, we might say, bloody-minded. The same word,
nabal, is used in Psalm 14:1: 'The fool says in his heart, "There is no God".'

The fool: obstinate, unwilling to listen and learn, quarrelsome and
with a mind firmly closed. Which of us would want to be described in
such a way? Who would want to admit to such behaviour? As we ponder
these different words, the different facets of foolishness they express and
the contexts in which each of them are used, it is all too easy to focus on
other people and think to ourselves, *Yes, I know people like that*. 'She never

---

14 I am indebted to Kidner for this analysis. Proverbs also refers to 'the simple' (Hebrew, *peti*) who are easily
led, gullible and downright silly (14:15), and 'the scoffer' (*les*), which occurs seventeen times. It is not that
that these sorts of people are stupid. It is about their attitude. They share with the fool their 'strong dislike
of correction' (9:7, 8; 13:1; 15:12).

listens.' 'He is so stubborn!' 'He is always trying to pick a fight.' 'He's not the brightest light bulb in the box.' 'She's just not interested in anyone's opinion but her own.'

Wouldn't the wiser path be for us to reflect on *our own* lives – on our attitudes and behaviours, and on the choices we make?

Choices

The choice between wisdom and folly is set before us clearly in Proverbs 9:13–18. The writer presents us with a picture of two houses. These houses are inhabited by two different women, one named 'Wisdom', and the other, 'Folly'. 'Wisdom is depicted as a noble patroness and Folly as a pretentious hostess.'[15] Each woman is calling out to the passers-by in the street, inviting them to enter her house for a meal. Both hostesses call out to 'the simple'; their invitations are issued to the same people.

Wisdom urges, 'Leave your simple ways and you will live; walk in the way of insight' (9:6). Choosing to enter the house of Wisdom will involve accepting rebuke and correction and growing in the knowledge of God (9:7–10).

By contrast, 'Folly is an unruly woman; she is simple and knows nothing' (9:13). She tries to lure people into her house, promising: 'Stolen water is sweet; food eaten in secret is delicious' (9:17). The writer adds the comment: 'But little do they know that the dead are there, that her guests are deep in the realm of the dead' (9:18).

So, here is the choice. Enter the house of Folly, which seems so attractive and which promises so much, yet which actually delivers nothing of value and leads to death. Or, enter the house of Wisdom and find life.

Jesus also offered this stark choice. In his famous parable of the wise man and the foolish man, Jesus describes the one who listens to his words as like a wise man who builds his house on rock. His house survives all the worst storms that come. The one who does not listen to the words of Jesus is like a fool who builds a house on sand, a house that is quickly destroyed in the first storm (Mt 7:24–27).

Wise or foolish? In his story, Jesus leaves us to ponder which we are, and what will be the outcomes of our choices. Proverbs makes the choice equally plain:

'For the waywardness of the simple will kill them, and the complacency of fools will destroy them; but whoever listens to me [Wisdom] will live in safety and be at ease, without fear of harm' (1:32–33).

---

15 Waltke, *Proverbs*, vol. 1, p. 429.

Reflection

1. Read the story of David, Nabal and his wife Abigail in 1 Samuel 25. What are the characteristics of foolishness displayed by Nabal? What were the results?
2. By contrast, what characteristics of wisdom are shown in a practical way by Abigail and with what effects?
3. According to the Bible, to try to live without acknowledging and honouring God our Creator is the ultimate foolishness (Ps 14:1). In what ways are you trying to live and work without reference to God?

9. HARD WORK, NOT LAZINESS

Read Proverbs 6:6–11 and 24:30–34

How long will you lie there, you sluggard? When will you get up
from sleep? A little sleep, a little slumber, a little folding of the
hands to rest – and poverty will come on you like a thief (6:9–10).

I recently listened to a talk in church, delivered to a group of 'millennials'.
The speaker was in his late twenties, dressed in shorts and a T-shirt, and
the title was 'Living a Balanced Life'. I assumed at first that this would be an
argument for the laid-back Aussie lifestyle, with a minimum of work and
effort and a maximum of relaxing on the beach and partying. Wrong! It
turned out to be a very wise and helpful biblical exposition about the virtue
of hard work and its value in God's sight.

Proverbs explores the value of work. It contrasts the attitude of the wise,
who work hard, save prudently and give generously, with the lazy. God
intends us to work and to support those who, for reasons of age, sickness,
disability or lack of opportunity, cannot work to support themselves.

The sluggard

Proverbs uses very direct, confronting language when attacking laziness:
'Go to the ant you sluggard; consider its ways and be wise! It has no
commander, no overseer or ruler, yet it stores its provisions in summer
and gathers its food at harvest' (6:6–8).

The hard work and instinctive foresight of ants is contrasted with the
lazy person, who never gives a thought to the future because they expects
someone else will provide for them. They are always wanting a little lie
down and never stir to make an effort: 'A little sleep, a little slumber, a
little folding of the hands to rest' (24:33).We might picture someone lazing
around on the couch at home, wasting hours flicking through the TV
channels, texting and tweeting about anything, but helping no-one and
producing nothing.

It also uses some humorous word pictures to make the point: 'As a door
turns on its hinges, so does a lazy person in bed. The lazy person buries a
hand in the dish, and is too tired to bring it back to the mouth (26:14–15,
NRSV). Not only are they too lazy to get out of bed in the morning, they
are too lazy even to make the effort to eat!

But there is a darker side to laziness; if you won't work, you will go hungry. 'Sluggards do not plough in season; so at harvest time they look but find nothing' (20:4). Poverty is also pictured as an unwelcome and threatening enemy who arrives when the lazy one least expects it: 'Poverty will come upon you like a robber, and want, like an armed warrior' (6:11, NRSV).

Hard work

Working hard, using our God-given gifts and energy, can be very enjoyable. We are, after all, made in the image of our Creator, which is why we find enjoyment in being creative and satisfaction in completing a task.

But often it is not so enjoyable. It's not much fun putting in a long shift on the production line, ironing clothes, dealing with difficult customers and demanding bosses, or juggling impossible deadlines and mindless bureaucracy. Work is tough for most people, but it is an essential part of God's way of providing for us and establishing and maintaining a functioning society. It is certainly a better option than hunger and poverty!

Proverbs mocks the sluggard's attitude and ridiculous excuses to avoid doing work. 'The sluggard says, "There's a lion outside! I'll be killed in the public square!"' (22:13). What sort of excuses do you hear at your home or workplace when people are trying to avoid doing a difficult job? Probably not as melodramatic as these! Perhaps, 'It's too hot', or, 'I'm not feeling up to it today' or, 'Why do I need to do that now?' Or, most commonly, 'It's not my job; why can't someone else do it?' The lazy person cannot expect others to do the work for them. At home, at work, wherever – we need to carry our share of the workload so far as we are capable of doing so.

The bigger picture

What if we want to work but can't? What if we have been made redundant? What if we are desperately looking for a job? Many of us will struggle with these situations at one time or another. Proverbs is generally silent on these issues, but the Bible as a whole has much to say to us in those situations about God's Fatherly care, his purpose for our lives and our need to trust him. It also calls those in work to encourage and support those struggling and in need.

What about the importance of rest and leisure? Again, Proverbs does not provide us with a comprehensive treatise on work and work–life balance. With the whole Bible in our hand, we know that God's plan from the very beginning was for us to rest from work one day in seven. Yes, we need time for worship, for studying God's word and prayer, for building relationships, for eating properly and exercising, for using our creative gifts and enjoying God's creation. But we are also to honour God in and through our work.

Proverbs doesn't paint a full picture of work and its value, but it does challenge the attitude we bring to our work and warns about the consequences of our choices. It leaves us with three clear truths about work and laziness:

- Work will bring wealth and put food on the table. Laziness will bring poverty and hunger.
- Laziness is a destroying negative in life, whereas work is a positive force needed to build up societies.
- We reap what we sow: as in farming, so in life.

'Lazy hands make for poverty, but diligent hands bring wealth' (10: 4).

Reflection

1. Read 1 Thessalonians 4:11–12 and 2 Thessalonians 3:6–15. What reasons does Paul give for valuing hard work?
2. Why do you think Paul needed to say such things?
3. Read Colossians 3:17–23. What does Paul teach us about our attitude to work today?

10. INTEGRITY, NOT DISHONESTY

Read Proverbs 11:1–11

The Lord detests dishonest scales, but accurate weights find
favour with him (11:1).

The integrity of the upright guides them, but the unfaithful are
destroyed by their duplicity (11:3).

Here is the third of the choices set out before us in Proverbs: the path
of integrity or the way of dishonesty. Proverbs has much to say about
integrity in relationships, being honest with people and being faithful
to our promises.[16] But a strong aspect of its focus is on integrity in our
commercial dealings and the way we handle money, and it is this aspect we
will explore here.

Cheating and shortcuts

I once worked for a public-sector authority where the top two leaders went
to jail for corruption. They were running a scam in which the authority
bought houses for its senior staff at artificially high prices, with a side
arrangement to share the large profit from the sale with the sellers (who
'just happened' to be friends of the bosses).

At the other end of the dishonesty spectrum to this sort of gross public
corruption are the under-the-counter cash payments required to get even
the simplest job done by public officials in many countries. A friend whose
work took him through several African countries described the time he
was stripped down to his underwear and held for nine hours because the
border guards wanted a bribe – which he steadfastly refused to offer!

We don't have to travel to other countries to face integrity choices every
day, whether in big ethical decisions in business or politics, or in simple
tests of honesty when we claim expenses and submit tax returns. There
is never a shortage of opportunities to be dishonest! Proverbs pictures
the thief 'winking the eyes, shuffling the feet, pointing the fingers, with
perverted mind devising evil, continually sowing discord' (6:13–14,
NRSV). It's a graphic picture of the ever-present temptation to 'make a
bit on the side', to get involved in a dishonest scheme, to take a shortcut to
financial gain.

---

16 See chapter 21 of this book.

We are left in no doubt that God hates it when we get involved in 'deceptive or misleading conduct'[17:] 'The LORD detests dishonest scales, but accurate weights find favour with him' (11:1). This message is repeated in slightly different forms to make sure we get the point: 'Differing weights and differing measures – the LORD detests them both' (20:10); and 'The LORD detests differing weights, and dishonest scales do not please him' (20:23).

The writer pictures the shopkeeper of a past generation using a balance to weigh out measures of grain. A dishonest dealer might use a weight that looked heavier than it was to 'balance' the grain, thus skimping on the customer's serve. Modern equivalents abound: the car dealer adjusting the odometer to deceive the buyer; the accountant who charges a client for five hours, when only four were spent on the work; the workers spending their employer's time on social media. Although such deceptive acts often go unchallenged, Proverbs hammers home the fact that God sees all our dealings.

But the LORD is not just watching; he is deeply involved in the process. If we cheat other people, we are also cheating God: 'Honest scales and balances belong to the LORD; all the weights in the bag are of his making' (16:11).

Integrity and faith

Faith in God needs to be matched by honesty. When we are dishonest, we are kidding ourselves that we won't be found out, that we won't be held to account and that there is no God who sees or cares.

Integity is not just a matter for individuals; it is cited as a core value of most major organisations and is a value generally admired in our society. So why do governments have to legislate to enforce it? Because without such regulatory oversight and intervention, human nature will tend to take the moral shortcut.

Proverbs is very realistic about human weakness and the deceptive attractiveness of dishonesty. It is also uncompromising about the importance and value of integrity. This is not just a side issue in our relationship with God; it is inextricably bound up with our professed faith: 'Whoever fears the LORD walks uprightly, but those who despise him are devious in their ways' (14:2).

---

17 This is a legal term used in the Australian Trade Practices Act.

Note the implicit assumption here, that integrity is a mark of someone who fears the LORD, and dishonesty is a mark of someone who shows by their actions a contemptuous disregard for God – whatever they profess to believe at church on Sundays.

I believe we are wise to read these proverbs, not so much as rules that condemn us, but as God's loving reminder that his way is best for us. If we are wise, we will remember them:

- when the path of dishonesty looks particularly attractive (20:17)
- when the temptation to take moral financial shortcuts seems overwhelming (21:6)
- when we are tempted to compromise our integrity and risk our reputation (22:1)
- when we are faced with the choice between making more money or retaining our integrity.

'Whoever walks in integrity walks securely, but whoever takes crooked paths will be found out' (10:9).

Reflection

1. What tests to honesty and integrity do you face in your daily life? What are your 'weak points'?
2. How do you equip yourself to face these tests?
3. How do you react when people lie, steal and cheat and seem to get away with it – and even prosper?

11. GENEROSITY, NOT EXPLOITATION

Read Proverbs 14:21–31 and 19:17

Whoever oppresses the poor shows contempt for their Maker, but
whoever is kind to the needy honours God (14:31).
Whoever is kind to the poor lends to the LORD, and he will reward
them for what they have done (19:17).

Taken together, these two proverbs sum up what God thinks about
exploitation of the poor on the one hand and generosity towards the poor
on the other.

A social conscience?

Exploitation of the poor and defenceless – widows, orphans and all victims
of injustice – is condemned everywhere in Scripture, not least in the book
of Proverbs. 'Do not exploit the poor because they are poor, and do not
crush the needy in court' (22:22, see also 28:3).

Here is a challenge to anyone entrusted with leadership, or with any
decision-making authority that affects the lives of others. We are not to use
the power granted to us to oppress or take advantage of others. We have
a duty of care, and we are accountable to God for this. We are to pay fair
wages, not the absolute minimum the market will bear. We are to apply the
'golden rule' (Lk 6:31) in our dealings and treat others as we would like to
be treated if we were in their situation.

What about the rest of us? We might say, 'I've never exploited anyone.
This doesn't apply to me.' We might criticise exploitation by others, but
be blind to how much we benefit from it ourselves. Take, for example,
merchandise produced in 'sweatshop' factories: we may feel indignant
watching a TV documentary about an exploitative business producing
training shoes at two dollars a pair, but we don't complain too loudly,
because we love to get a bargain!

On the other side of the coin, Proverbs tells us that care for the poor is
a hallmark of righteousness, of being in right relationship with God and
living to please him: 'The righteous care about justice for the poor, but
the wicked have no such concern' (29:7). Indeed, generosity of spirit is a
hallmark of a wise and godly man or woman. It springs from more than
a social conscience. This sort of generosity flows from understanding and
enjoying God's goodness to us. It is a part of our covenant obligation and a

condition of God's prospering us.

Faith and money

These proverbs draw a strong connection between the use of money and a person's relationship with God. They expose how the selfish and self-centred attitudes that underlie our unwillingness to care for the poor show what we really think about God: 'Whoever mocks the poor shows contempt for their Maker' (17:5). By contrast, kindness to the poor is like 'lending to the LORD'.

Jesus spoke a lot about money as a great servant but a terrible master, and about the particular temptations that come to the rich. The problem is that most of us don't consider ourselves as rich at all. Our definition of rich usually includes 'anyone with more money than me!' But the warnings in Scripture therefore apply to all of us. It has been shrewdly observed that a change in attitude towards money is one of the clearest indicators that God is at work in a person's life. God has a way of loosening our grips on our wallets and possessions and changing us into more generous and caring people (see 2 Cor 9:6–8).

Money and power: both can be used for ill or for good. Proverbs explicitly condemns exploitation of the poor and disadvantaged. But generosity and concern for those in need are characteristics of God, and therefore bring the blessing of God. 'Those who give to the poor will lack nothing, but those who close their eyes to them receive many curses' (28:27).

Exploitation or generosity. Which will you choose?

Reflection

1. Take a check on the way you exercise any position of authority you may hold (at work, in the community or in the home). In what ways are you tempted to abuse that power?
2. If someone knew nothing about your professed faith, what would they learn about you from the way you treat people in need and the way you use your money?
3. Read 2 Corinthians 8. What do you learn here about generosity and sharing of God-given wealth?

12. HUMILITY, NOT SELF-PROMOTION

Read Proverbs 25:6–7

Do not exalt yourself in the king's presence, and do not claim a
place among his great men (25:6).

The word 'narcissism' has come back into common speech in recent years.
It is frequently used to describe self-absorbed politicians, business leaders
and celebrities, the 'media tarts', the people who always demand to be at the
centre of attention and those obsessed with their own image. 'Positioning',
as a personal marketing strategy, now plays out on social media profiles.
Whatever social circles we move in, we seem to feel the need for people to
see us in the best possible light. We naturally want people to think well of
us.

It's not all about me

There is a better way to live, one modelled and taught by Jesus, which frees
us from the frantic need to continually promote ourselves.

But how are we to apply this teaching in a culture that requires us to
draw attention to our qualifications and achievements in order to get
work? Anyone who has ever applied for a job and attended a job interview
has engaged in self-promotion of a sort. However we dress it up, a well-
written and well-presented CV is designed to say to the reader: 'Look what
I have done! Look how clever I am!' A company positions itself to sell its
products. Aspiring politicians promote themselves to get elected. Those
trying to climb the corporate ladder seemingly must promote themselves
to succeed.

As Alexander Hill asks: 'Is there a place for humble people in the
corporate world today? Or are they victims-in-waiting, the next road kill
on the capitalist highway?'[18]

There is a fine line somewhere between presenting our skills and
services in a competitive market and drawing constant and unnecessary
attention to ourselves and our achievements. I suspect that where this line
is drawn varies between people, depending on our personality types, how
competitive we are and whether we are extroverted or introverted. I may
not always be sure where to draw that line, but I usually know when I have
crossed it!

---

18 Hill, *Just Business*, p. 30.

Jockeying for position

Proverbs gives us clear guidance to navigate this tricky issue. It warns us not to focus on self-positoning: 'Do not exalt yourself in the king's presence, and do not claim a place among his great men; it is better for him to say to you, "Come up here," than for him to humiliate you before his nobles' (25:6–7).

Scrambling for position in the halls of power is not an attractive game to play or watch. Allow others to draw attention to your worth instead: 'Let someone else praise you, and not your own lips'(27:2).

Jesus made a very similar point. He observed the common social behaviour of guests at a big dinner party trying to position themselves in the best seats – a behaviour pattern very often observable today. Attend any political or business function, or even some church or social functions, and watch the upwardly mobile 'work the room' to position themselves near to those they deem as important to the progress of their career or social status. Watch them look over your shoulder as they are talking to you to see if there is someone more important they should be moving on to meet. So, Jesus tells his audience, in words reminiscent of Proverbs, and in a nice combination of principle and pragmatism:

> 'When someone invites you to a wedding feast, do not take the place
> of honour, for a person more distinguished than you may have been
> invited. If so, the host who invited both of you will come and say to
> you, "Give this person your seat." Then, humiliated, you will have
> to take the least important place. But when you are invited, take
> the lowest place so that you're your host comes, he will say to you,
> "Friend, move up to a better place"' (Lk 14:7–10).

Perhaps surprisingly, Jesus does not condemn recognition of status here. Rather, he condemns grasping for that status ourselves.

Handling Success

One of the tests of wisdom and humility is how we handle success. Naturally we enjoy success when it comes, but do we then grab all the glory and attention and awards going around for ourselves and conveniently forget the contributions of others, or do we acknowledge and celebrate the contributions of others and our dependence on them and on God?

We lack humility when we chase success for its own sake, like a drug, to satisfy our craving for the adulation of others: 'It is not good to eat much honey, or to seek honour on top of honour' (25:27, NRSV). Both result in a 'sickening effect of over-indulgence'.[19] We don't feel good about ourselves afterwards.

We lack humility when we are blind to our own weaknesses and rate our ideas and abilities as being much better than anyone else's: 'Do you see a person wise in their own eyes? There is more hope for a fool than for them' (26:12).

We lack humility when we get an inflated sense of our own importance: 'The crucible for silver and the furnace for gold, but man is tested by the praise he receives' (27:21, NRSV). Very few of us handle success well.

True humility is impossible to counterfeit. It is unrelated to role or position. I have met very humble leaders and very proud underlings, and vice versa. Humility is a right understanding of ourselves in relation to God and others. In an increasingly self-absorbed society, it is a stand-out quality.

C.S. Lewis, in writing about pride as 'the great sin', described a truly humble person in these words, 'He will not be thinking about humility; he will not be thinking about himself at all.'[20]

Reflection

Read Romans 12 and notice the teaching about humility.

1. Why does Paul emphasise so strongly the need for a right understanding of ourselves in relation to others? (12:3).

2. In what practical ways can you apply verse 10: 'Honour one another above yourselves'; and verse 16: 'Do not be proud, but be willing to associate with people of low position. Do not be conceited'?

---

19   Moss, *Proverbs*, p. 116.
20   Lewis, *Mere Christianity*, p. 112.

13. TRUST IN GOD, NOT SELF-RELIANCE

Read Proverbs 16:1–25 and 19:20–23

In their hearts humans plan their course, but the LORD establishes
their steps (16:9).
Many are the plans in a person's heart, but it is the LORD's purpose
that prevails (19:21).

We may make our plans, but God is ultimately in charge. So how do we
know which of our plans are just our bright ideas and which are in line
with God's will?

The path is always clearer looking back. Looking ahead, it may seem
blocked, difficult or uncertain. How do we choose 'the right way' when we
are faced with so many options? How do we know where we should live,
what work we should do or which person to marry? How do we experience
the guidance of God? In our planning and decision making, are we meant
to rely on our God-given abilities to think, reason and plan, and to assess
likely outcomes, or are we meant to pray and leave it all to God?

Guidance

The Bible shows us that God may choose to guide us in 'special' ways:
through dreams, through a prophetic message, through an unusually strong
inner conviction or through the wise, unequivocal counsel of another. We
find examples of all of these in the Bible.

Some would try to present these as the normal means of God's guidance,
and imply that anything less is unspiritual. But this would be contrary to
Scripture, and contrary to the experience of the apostles as recorded in the
book of Acts and the New Testament letters.

The Apostle Paul was guided in a dream to undertake missionary work
in Macedonia (Acts 16:9–10) and on another occasion received a message
through a dream that he should stay in Corinth (Acts 18:9–10). But
most of his decision making during his missionary travels involved more
apparently ordinary factors such as personal choice, requests from fellow
believers, inner conviction or opportune circumstances.

This mix of the obviously supernatural and the seemingly normal runs
right through Scripture. We find Elisha being miraculously delivered by
the unseen heavenly forces camped around him (2 Kgs 6:17), but on a
subsequent occasion he tells his servant to barricade the doors when he

was under attack (6:32). Peter gets released from prison through the work of angels opening the doors (Acts 12:6–10), but when he gets home he knocks at the closed door to get in; he doesn't pray for supernatural help to open that door!

No explanation is offered as to why God chooses to show his supernatural power on some occasions or why he works through ordinary human processes at other times. We don't know why. God has not told us.

Proverbs and practicalities

Proverbs doesn't tell us much about *how* God guides us. Rather, it provides us with clear reasons for trusting that God *will* guide us and gives some unchanging principles to help us move forward with confidence. It is more concerned with practicalities than speculation.

First, Proverbs reminds us that God promises to guide us as we commit our decisions and plans to him. As we trust in him, choosing not to rely solely on our own knowledge and wisdom, he will direct us (3:5–6).

Second, Proverbs warns us that our own wits and resources are insufficient without God's wisdom and insight: 'There is a way that appears to be right, but in the end it leads to death' (14:12; 16:25). God sees the underlying motives of our hearts: 'All a person's ways seem pure to them, but motives are weighed by the LORD' (16:2).

Third, Proverbs encourages us to pray about all our plans before, during and after we make key decisions, secure in the knowledge that God will work out his loving purpose in our lives: 'In their hearts humans plan their course, but the LORD establishes their steps' (16:9).

In all of this, Proverbs reminds us that God is sovereign. He is in charge. And yet, woven into God's plans, we make our plans and decisions and are accountable for them.

Sometimes we may mistakenly think that God is only engaged in our lives when we choose to consult him. We may live for long periods without giving God a thought. Then, when we have a big decision to make, we pray. When we get sick, we pray for healing. When we have money worries, we ask God for help. When we get into a dangerous situation we ask God to protect us. Thanks to God that, in his grace, he may answer those prayers and use such experiences of need to get our attention. But let us remember: he is Almighty God, not an on-call security, health or financial advisory service for times of need!

If we are wise, we pray for guidance as we plan rather than rely solely on our own resources. If we are wise, we look to God to guide us as we work out our plans, and we trust him for the outcomes. If we are wise, we make trusting God a way of life.

Reflection

1. What big decisions are you facing right now? Read Proverbs 3:5–6. Make these wise words the basis of your prayers and plans and decisions.
2. Read Jesus' words about trusting rather than worrying about the basics of life (Mt 6:25–34) or fearing about life-and-death issues (Jn 14:1–4). What worries are crowding into your life right now? How do Jesus' words' help you deal with them?

14. INWARD PURITY,
NOT OUTWARD PIETY

Read Proverbs 4:20–23 and 20:5–9

Who can say, 'I have kept my heart pure;
I am clean and without sin'? (20:9).

Proverbs majors on the practical – how we actually live and what we say and do. But it is nonetheless interested in what goes on deep within us: 'The purposes of a person's heart are deep waters, but one who has insight draws them out' (20:5). As the writer reflects further, he realises that the 'deep waters' are murky, to say the least. He asks (rhetorically): 'Who can say, 'I have kept my heart pure; I am clean and without sin'? (20:9). The problem with our impure hearts is that they show themselves in impure behaviour. What is inside has to come out eventually, however much we might try to cover it up.

The gap

There is a gap between how we like people to think of us and what we are really like. Professing faith in God and claiming to live a good life is one thing, but the reality may be quite another: 'Many claim to have unfailing love, but a faithful person who can find?' (20:6).

It seems like the writer of Psalm 20 has been let down by a friend or business partner, or perhaps a marriage partner, who claimed to be loyal but failed to keep their promises.

If we have been through bad experiences where people have let us down, or if we have become disillusioned with Christians who have broken their promises and Christian churches that have failed to live up the standards of Christ, let's just remember that all of us wrestle with this problem of sinful hearts. When we try to live out what we profess to believe, we often fail. Even the Apostle Paul experienced that (see Rom 7:15–20). How do we deal with the problem? The normal human response is to cover up, to paper over the cracks with an veneer of morality or reliance on religious ceremony. Neither fixes the problem.

The wise path is honesty, not hypocrisy.

Religion or reality?

Jesus made enemies of the Pharisees, the ultra-religious right of his day, because he exposed them for the hypocrites they were. Like many religions of our day, the Judaism of the Pharisees had extensive laws about food and drink and how to prepare it, and strict rules about washing utensils and dishes. The Pharisees' focus was on outward ceremony, rather than the state of their hearts and their need of God's grace. Jesus latched onto their obsession with only taking 'pure things' into their body and their narrow focus on ceremonial laws. They had missed the big point: it is the sin in our hearts that defiles and makes us filthy, not the food and drink we take into our bodies.

Jesus said: 'Don't you see that whatever enters the mouth goes into the stomach and then out of the body? But the things that come out of a person's mouth come from the heart, and these defile them. For out of the heart come evil thoughts – murder, adultery, sexual immorality, theft, false testimony, slander. These are what defile a person' (Mt 15:16–19).

This is not just New Testament teaching; we find it throughout the Bible. An example is Samuel's rebuke of King Saul (1 Sam 15:22–23). God sees into our hearts. Therefore, we need to be made clean on the inside. True religion is not primarily about outward ceremonies. We need a change of heart, a new heart, and this is what God has promised to give us: 'I will give you a new heart and put a new spirit within you' (Ezek 36:26).

Guard your heart

Surprisingly, perhaps, for a book so focused on outward behaviour, Proverbs zeroes in on this core human problem, the problem of the human heart: 'Above all else, guard your heart, for everything you do flows from it' (Prov 4:23).

This saying comes after the urgent command to listen, to 'pay attention to what I say' (4:20). By listening, the writer means giving our full attention. This is not the distracted kind of listening that we do when we switch on the radio while driving in the car. Nor is it like listening to a lecture, where we may sift the information for what we think is relevant to us, make our notes and ignore the rest. He means that we are to take all of God's wise words into our minds and hearts: 'Do not let them out of your sight, *keep them within your heart*; for they are like life to those who find them and health to one's whole body' (4:21–22, italics mine).

I've recently taken up Pilates. It's good for me because my physical 'core' needs strengthening to maintain flexibility and balance. When my inner core is weak, then other parts of the body try to compensate and all sorts of aches and strains start to occur. It's the inner core that needs strengthening.

So it is with our lives. God's truth is not just intended for the mind. It is a powerful, life-giving seed, intended to take root at the very centre of our beings. We need purity and strength on the inside. We need for God to deal with our deepest problem – our sin – through recognising and accepting that Jesus Christ died for us (1 Pet 2:24; Rom 5:6–8) and through receiving the gift of his Holy Spirit.

The honesty of the book of Proverbs demands that we look inside ourselves at our desires, our motives and our relationship with God, as well as at our outward behaviour.

'Above all else, guard your heart, for everything you do flows from it.'

Reflection

1. 'You hypocrites! You do not practise what you preach!' This is one of the most common criticisms of religious people in any culture. Think about your life. Where might this charge apply to you?
2. Read Psalm 51:10 and Psalm 86:11. Turn these into your prayer.
3. Proverbs 20:6 notes the rare quality of faithfulness. Why does the writer value this so highly, and why is it so rare?

15. JUSTICE, NOT PRIVATE RELIGION

Read Proverbs 31:8–9

Speak up for those who cannot speak for themselves, for the rights
of all who are destitute. Speak up and judge fairly; defend the
rights of the poor and needy (31:8–9).

In the face of injustice, silence and inaction are a sin.

We all have a duty of care: for those who cannot care for themselves,
for those who are not getting a fair deal, for those without the resources or
ability to speak for themselves.

If we turn religion into a purely private affair, divorced from any
wider concerns about the state of the world and the desperate need of the
majority, then we are closing our ears to the word of God, which speaks
very loudly about injustice: 'If anyone turns a deaf ear to my instruction,
even their prayers are detestable' (28:9). If we will not heed the word of
God about how we live and relate to one another, then there is no point in
engaging in any 'religious activity' such as prayer and worship. God will
not listen to our prayers or accept our worship.

Worship and justice

In making this point, Proverbs is very much in line with the prophets of the
Old Testament. Amos, speaking the word of God to a corrupt, complacent,
unjust society that loved to keep up the religious traditions and celebrate
the ancient feasts, proclaimed: 'I hate, I despise your religious festivals;
your assemblies are a stench to me. Even though you bring me burnt
offerings and grain offerings, I will not accept them. Though you bring
choice fellowship offerings, I will have no regard for them. Away with the
noise of your songs! I will not listen to the music of your harps. But let
justice roll on like a river, righteousness like a never failing stream!' (Amos
5:21–24).

What was the problem? In Amos's day, there was public worship with
lots of music and singing, and with big crowds in attendance. Religion
seemed to be going well, but greed was doing even better. The gap between
rich and poor was increasing, as in so many countries today, and there was
no fair deal for the poor or those who couldn't afford to pay the lawyers
or bribe judges. The people's greed, complacency and neglect of their
responsibilities to the poor were described as both offences against the

law of God and as sin against God himself. God was not deceived by the religious façade. He saw what was really going on: 'For I know how many are your offences and how great your sins' (Amos 5:12). He saw, and he was holding the people accountable.

We are a consumer society in which it is easy to let our worship of God become like an entertainment event in the weekly schedule. The possibility that God may not accept our worship is alien to popular Western culture. If we are in the minority of people who go to church to worship, then we expect to be rewarded and, to a point, entertained. If we are giving up our valuable leisure time, then we expect something in return: an interesting talk (though not too long!), good music, friendly and interesting people and a comfortable building. But Proverbs, in line with the prophets, warns us that if our lives show no concern for injustice or the welfare of the poor, then it is not a case of whether we find the worship event acceptable to us, but *whether God finds our worship acceptable to him.*

Transformed societies

The world would be a much poorer place without those who have stood up for the cause of the oppressed and powerless. We only need think of people like William Wilberforce, who worked most of his adult life to see slavery abolished in the British Empire; Lord Shaftesbury, the nineteenth-century reformer who campaigned successfully against the horrific exploitation of child labour; or Elizabeth Fry, known as 'the angel of prisons' for her work in improving the awful prison conditions of the same period. All three were Christians whose faith led them to show the compassion of God in practical ways. They all made a lasting difference for good on a national and international scale. All three lived out God's call to us in the book of Proverbs, to 'speak up for those who cannot speak for themselves', to speak up for the destitute, to defend the rights of the poor and needy.

Thank God, there are thousands of more recent examples: those who have founded child protection agencies, organised and contributed to famine relief, founded and served in medical hospitals and refugee camps and helped street kids in the slums of the world's cities get an education and opportunity to work.

The challenge for us here is not just to stand back and applaud the efforts of others. It is to ask ourselves in what ways we can speak up for those who have no voice. It may be assisting an elderly house-bound person claim their rightful benefits, helping a new immigrant who is being exploited by an unscrupulous landlord, or pursuing an injustice through the courts or political processes. We might need to stand up for a colleague at work who is being unfairly treated and not able to stand up for themselves. Proverbs presents God's call for us to do *something* that links our professed faith to justice in society.

In our increasingly secular society, we can't allow ourselves to succumb to the pressure to make Christian faith a purely private affair. Jesus told us to 'let your light shine before others so that they may see your good deeds and glorify your Father in heaven' (Mt 5:16).

Reflection

1. In what ways can you speak and act for justice in your workplace and community?
2. In what practical ways can you help the poor?
3. When you next take part in a public worship service, how can you best prepare to offer worship acceptable to God? (Ps 139: 23, 24; 1 Cor 11:28).

COMMUNICATION

True wisdom comes through in how, and what, we communicate. Most of us know what it is like to blurt something out, only to regret it later, or to send an email and immediately reach for the recall. Information, photos and messages posted on the internet may be very difficult to remove.

We might be able to recall emails if we are quick enough and have the right system, but spoken words come out of the mouth like toothpaste from a tube, and we can never put them back in.

Proverbs has much to teach us about wise communication: about our spoken and written words, about the wisdom of remaining silent, about listening and learning from others and about resolving conflict situations.

16. WISE WORDS

Read Proverbs 15:1–7

The tongue of the wise adorns knowledge, but the mouth of the
fool gushes folly (15:2).

We had moved countries and were trying to find a house to live in. Things
were not going well. I felt loaded down with worries and the way forward
was cloudy.

I was sharing my problems at length with an older friend over a coffee.
After listening carefully, he said gently, 'I think the God who made the
universe has that particular problem under control, don't you? Let's pray
about it now.' In other circmstances, that sort of reply might have sounded
trite. In that particluar situation, they were wise words indeed, and they
changed my whole mood and outlook.

Proverbs says much about speaking wisely; it also warns us about
foolish talk.

Wise words: positive and powerful

The wise person knows *when* to speak and when to keep silent: 'Sin is not
ended by multiplying words, but the prudent hold their tongues' (10:19).

The wise person knows *what* to say when they opens their mouths:
'The hearts of the wise make their mouths prudent, and their lips promote
instruction' (16:23).

The wise person knows the *right time* to say the *right thing*. There
are moments to teach and rebuke, and moments to offer a quiet word of
encouragement. Unwise and untimely words can be very damaging. By
contrast, wise words spoken at the right time, particularly to those facing
crisis situations, are more valuable and beautiful than the most expensive
jewellery (20:15).

What are the characteristics of wise words? They have a lasting
significance: 'Truthful lips endure forever, but a lying tongue lasts only
a moment' (12:19). We are thinking about these proverbs nearly three
thousand years after they were written! Wise words are informative: 'The
lips of the wise spread knowledge; but the hearts of fools are not upright'
(15:7); they are also constructive, even in rebuke: 'Like an earring of gold
or an ornament of fine gold is the rebuke of a wise judge to a listening ear'
(25:12).

Wise words bring healing to wounded people: 'The words of the reckless pierce like swords, but the tongue of the wise brings healing' (12:18). They build up: 'The lips of the righteous nourish many' (10:21); they relieve worry: 'Anxiety weighs down the heart, but a kind word cheers it up' (12:25); and they defuse tension: 'A gentle answer turns away wrath, but a harsh word stirs up anger' (15:1).

Proverbs gives us word pictures to describe the very positive effect that wise words can have on others: 'An honest answer is like a kiss on the lips' (24:26) and 'Like apples of gold in settings of silver is a ruling rightly given' (25:11).

Foolish talk: negative and destructive

In contrast, Proverbs warns us about foolish talk and its effects. I once attended a work social function where the organiser had booked a comedian. After the usual predictable jokes about the bosses, he decided to make some unsavoury jokes about gay people. One of my staff at the time was gay. Half of the audience, including myself, got up and walked out in protest. The comedian, realising he had self-destructed, also cut short his performance and left. The evening was memorable, but for the wrong reasons. It was an example of particularly unwise talk.

Foolish talk includes much more than bad jokes. In Proverbs we find several examples of unwise words and their effects. Unwise words lie and flatter: 'A lying tongue hates those it hurts, and a flattering mouth works ruin' (26:28). They deceive: 'Do not testify against your neighbour without cause – would you use your lips to deceive? Do not say, "I'll do to them as they have done to me; I'll pay them back for what they did."' (24:28–29).

Unwise words cut people down: 'With their mouths the godless destroy their neighbours' (11:9). They also spread gossip and betray: 'The words of a gossip are like choice morsels; they go down to the inmost parts' (18:9); and 'A gossip betrays a confidence but a trustworthy man keeps a secret' (11:13).

Unwise words destroy relationships: 'A perverse person stirs up conflict and a gossip separates close friends' (16:28); and they fuel strife and discontent: 'Without wood a fire goes out; without gossip a quarrel dies down. As charcoal to embers and as wood to fire, so is a quarrelsome person for kindling strife' (26:20–21).

Knowing the damage we can do with foolish talk, and the good we can do with wise words, perhaps we should make these words part of our daily prayers: 'Set a guard over my mouth, LORD; keep watch over the door of my lips' (Ps 141:3).

Or, as the Psalmist might have written in the twenty-first century: 'Set a guard, LORD, over my smart phone, laptop and tablet. Keep watch over my phone calls, texts, Facebook posts, emails and tweets'!

Reflection

1. What is the wisest advice you have ever been given?
2. Think back over your life and thank God for those who have spoken or written words that that have encouraged, corrected, challenged or inspired you.
3. Can you help someone today by what you say and the messages you send?

17. GOLDEN SILENCE

Read Proverbs 10:11–21 and 18:2–13

Sin is not ended by multiplying words, but the prudent hold
their tongues (10:19).

Jesus knew the wisdom of silence.

The first recorded teaching of Jesus, in Luke's Gospel, is in a synagogue in
his hometown of Nazareth. After Jesus had finished reading and preaching
from Isaiah 61, Luke observes, 'All spoke well of him and were amazed at
the gracious words that came from his lips' (Lk 4:22). It was not just the
miracles he performed that amazed the people; it was also the wisdom and
penetrating insight of his words.

But Jesus, in his great wisdom, also knew the value of silence. He knew
when there was nothing more to be said. He knew to stay silent when he
stood before Pilate, the Roman governor who condemned him to death
(Mt 27:14).

The book of Proverbs places a high value on silence – at the right time.
It helps us understand those situations when silence is the right response.
That wise Old Testament book of Ecclesiastes puts it like this: 'There is a
time for everything, and a season for every activity under the heavens ... a
time to be silent and a time to speak (Eccl 3:1, 7).

'A time to be silent'

Silence is wise when someone else is speaking. We should listen before
we blurt out our opinions: 'To answer before listening – that is folly and
shame' (Prov 18:13) and 'Fools find no pleasure in understanding but
delight in airing their own opinions' (18:2).

Silence is appropriate when we are ignorant of the subject being
discussed. We don't have to express an opinion about everything! 'Even
fools are thought wise if they keep silent, and discerning if they hold their
tongues' (17:28).

Going into a work meeting, a colleague advised me (tongue-in-cheek),
'Far better to keep silent and be thought a fool than to open your mouth
and remove all doubt.' Sounds like a good proverb! I have learned that not
everyone who asks me a question wants to hear my answer. I may need to
keep my mouth shut and listen further in order to understand what lies
behind the question before I launch into giving my opinions.

Silence is best when we have nothing useful or helpful or kind to add to the conversation, or when our words will simply be adding fuel to the flame: 'Whoever derides their neighbour has no sense, but the one who has understanding holds their tongue' (11:12).

If we get involved in a robust conversation where we are starting to say things that we will later regret, we become aware of a choice, one that requires us to make a decision in a split second: do we jump in and inflame a situation or do we stay silent, walk away and do and say something more productive? 'Sin is not ended by multiplying words, but the prudent hold their tongues' (10:19).

Silence is often the most compassionate response when people are pouring out their grief to us. 'Like one who takes away a garment on a cold day, or like vinegar poured on a wound, is one who sings songs to a heavy heart' (25:20). Job's comforters did very little right in helping Job understand the reasons for his suffering. Perhaps the most helpful thing of all was their silent show of support when they first arrived, as they sat with him on the ground for seven days and seven nights: 'No one said a word to him, because they saw how great his suffering was' (Job 2:13).

An American member of our church in Australia went through a nightmare experience with international bureaucracy when she and her husband adopted a baby girl from China. Sitting alone in a United States immigration office, after yet another setback, separated from her husband and children who were back in Australia, she wrote these words:

> I would like to think this pain has changed me, and I will comfort others differently than I did before. I will not rush friends to the other side of challenging circumstances so quickly with quickly spouted verses. I won't judge someone's spirituality based on how quickly they can bounce back. Instead, I'll sit with others in their pain, in their desperation, and say, 'You *are* me and your pain is my pain. Let's walk through all its intricacies and feel every part of it, and eventually we'll come out on the other side, but there is no rush. Take as long as you need.' I can't say I've always been a safe place for others' pain, but I pray that now, by God's grace, I am.[21]

'Slow to speak'

The New Testament letter of James contains practical wisdom very similar to Proverbs, particularly in this matter of what we say, and when and how

---

21 Phillips, *Bringing Lucy Home*, p. 109.

we say it: 'My dear brothers and sisters, take note of this. Everyone should be quick to listen, slow to speak and slow to become angry' (Jas 1:19).

Back in Proverbs, we learn that remaining silent allows us to stop and engage our brains before we speak: 'The tongue of the wise adorns knowledge, but the mouth of the fool gushes folly' (15:2). This slowness to speak keeps us from 'foot-in-mouth disease'. It holds us back from unnecessary trouble: 'Those who guard their mouths and their tongues keep themselves from calamity' (21:23) and, 'Those who guard their lips preserve their lives, but those who speak rashly will come to ruin' (13:3).

Finally, silence is a worthy response when people have no desire for truth and constructive discussion but are just playing power games to suit their own agenda. When the Pharisees brought to Jesus a woman caught in the act of adultery, Jesus could see that they were just using the poor woman for their own ends of trapping him into undermining the law. He could see their hatred for him. His first response was silence: he said nothing, instead bending down to write (what did he write?) in the sand with his finger (Jn 8:6).

Here is a lesson for us. We don't have to respond immediately to every question we are asked. We don't have to fit in with the agenda of people who just want to score points or argue about obscure points of faith rather than seriously open their hearts and minds to God's truth. In these circumstances, there is nothing we can say that will add value to the situation.

Sometimes, silence is the wisest response. Sometimes, silence is golden.

Reflection

1. How can you best avoid, or help defuse, situations where an unhelpful argument is a likely outcome?
2. In what circumstances is silence a constructive rather than a negative response? See, for example, Proverbs 11:13.
3. When you know you are going into a difficult meeting at work, or when an argument breaks out at home, try praying this 'arrow prayer': 'Set a guard over my mouth, LORD; keep watch over the door of my lips' (Ps 141:3).

18. LISTENING AND LEARNING

Read Proverbs 4:1–22

My child, be attentive to my words; incline your ear to my sayings.
Do not let them escape from your sight; keep them within your
heart. For they are life to those who find them, and healing to all
their flesh (4:20–22, NRSV).

In a large machinery repair workshop in southern Tanzania, where I once worked, the foreman posted this notice in large print on the wall: *Kuuliza si wajinga. Si kuuliza ni.* It translates: 'To ask is not stupidity. Not to ask is.'

This sign was there for the benefit of the workshop apprentices, who may have felt reluctant to show their ignorance about a particular system or procedure. It was there to encourage a workplace culture of learning and discourage a 'know-it-all' attitude, which, in an engineering workshop, is not just unhelpful; it can be downright dangerous.

Willingness to listen

Proverbs emphasises the wisdom of a willingness to listen and learn. Right from the beginning, it tells us to listen to the words of the wise (1:5), listen to our parents (1:8) and learn to reverence God (1:7). Then discretion will protect us, and understanding will guard us (2:11). It is only fools who despise wisdom and instruction (1:7).

The whole of chapter 4 is a plea to listen and learn: to listen to our parents (4:1, 4, 10, 20), to get hold of wisdom (4:5), and to guard it (4:13) and value it (4:8). It will beautify our lives (4:9) and lead us up a path of increasing understanding and satisfaction: 'The path of the righteous is like the morning sun, shining ever brighter till the full light of day' (4:18).

The call to listen comes repeatedly through the book. Indeed, this instruction seems to introduce a new section of writing each time that it occurs in the first 10 chapters:

- 'Hear, my child, your father's instruction, and do not reject your mother's teaching (1:8).
- 'My child, if you accept my words and treasure up my commandments within you... ' (2:1).
- 'My child, do not forget my teaching' (3:1).
- 'Listen, children, to a father's instruction' (4:1).

- 'My child, be attentive to my wisdom; incline your ear to my understanding' (5:1).
- 'My child, keep your father's commandment, and do not forsake your mother's teaching' (6:20).
- 'My child, keep my words and store up my commandments with you' (7:1).
- 'And now, my children, listen to me' (8:32).[22]

I think we get the message!

There seems to be a disease afflicting some people who get promoted into senior positions in politics, business and academia, and even in the church. The visible symptoms are that the new leader no longer thinks that anything worthwhile is happening unless they are doing the talking. I shared a dinner table recently with a business leader who talked at great length and then played with his mobile phone while anyone else was talking. I was not the only one who noticed! It was obviously discourteous behaviour, but is was also a symptom of such an overweening pride that the person in question no longer thought he could learn anything of value from those around him. He was no longer willing to even offer the simple courtesy of listening. Proverbs describes this sort of behaviour with brutal honesty: 'Fools find no pleasure in understanding but delight in airing their own opinions' (18:2).

Active listening

Listening is serious business. Willingness to listen is a mark of a good leader, and readiness to listen to your children is certainly a mark of good parenting. Proverbs warns that failure to listen could even ruin your life: 'Since they would not accept my advice and spurned my rebuke, they will eat the fruit of their ways and be filled with the fruit of their schemes. For the waywardness of the simple will kill them, and the complacency of fools will destroy them' (1:20–32).

In contrast, the ability to listen brings protection: 'Whoever listens to me will live in safety and be at ease, without fear of harm' (1:33). Furthermore, those who listen to rebuke and discipline grow wise: 'Like an earring of gold or an ornament of fine gold is the rebuke of a wise judge to a listening ear' (25:12) and, 'Whoever heeds a life-giving correction will be at home among the wise' (15:31).

Over the past ten years, the widespread use of smartphones and tablets has placed a great strain on conversation. We face the temptation to

---

22   All of these quotations are from the NRSV.

multitask during meetings, in gatherings with family and friends and even at mealtimes! Perhaps we need to rediscover the art of active, respectful listening to others, together with the humility to accept that others may have something to say that is worth listening to. The writer of Proverbs puts it in the bluntest of terms: 'The way of fools seems right to them, but the wise listen to advice' (12:15).

Reflection

1. How can you become a better listener?
2. Who do you find it hardest to take advice and instruction from: A parent? Spouse? Boss? Best friend? Why is that?
3. What steps can you take to listen more to God's word? Ask God to help you listen more, think more and speak less.

WISDOM AND RELATIONSHIPS

We don't exercise wisdom in isolation; it is not a private matter. As we have seen, it is much more than the ability to think wise thoughts, make wise decisions and do wise things. Wisdom is exercised through building loving relationships in the home, developing respect and integrity in the workplace and learning to deal with conflict. Above all, it is rooted in reverence for God and in the knowledge of him.

19. A RELATIONSHIP WITH GOD

Read Proverbs 9:10

The fear of the LORD is the beginning of wisdom, and knowledge
of the Holy One is understanding (9:10).

Fear of God: this is the source and basis of true wisdom. In Proverbs, the
'fear of the LORD' is found in the first chapter, and in the last. It is a major
theme that runs right through the book. As we shall see in the second part
of this book, it is also a major theme in the Psalms.

Knowing God

The 'fear of the LORD' is linked to knowing the LORD: not knowledge *about*
the LORD, but intimate knowledge *of* him, a spiritual relationship that
comes through faith in God's word to humankind.

But if the framework for the book of Proverbs is a covenant relationship
between the LORD and the believer – and it is – then what exactly is meant
by fear? In what sense are we to 'fear the LORD'?

The 'fear of the LORD' is much more than respect. It is a deeper
knowledge than a passing nod to the Almighty on the occasional Sunday,
or a desperate search in the dark in a time of crisis. It is an intimate
relationship with God.

Proverbs drives home to us the benefits of this kind of relationship
with God. The 'fear of the LORD' leads to *safety*: 'Whoever fears the LORD
has a secure fortress, and for their children it will be a refuge' (14:26); to
deliverance from evil: 'Through the fear of the LORD evil is avoided' (16:6);
to *life*: 'The fear of the LORD is a fountain of life, turning a person from
the snares of death' (14:27); and to *contentment*: 'Better a little with fear of
the LORD than great wealth with turmoil' (15:16). The 'fear of the LORD' is
more important than the fear of other people: 'Fear of man will prove to be
a snare, but whoever trusts in the LORD is kept safe' (29:25).

Love and fear

However, although the 'fear of the LORD' is the *beginning* of wisdom, it is
not the *end* of wisdom. It is not the whole story. Why? Because the wisdom
of God includes the love of God. 'The LORD is compassionate and gracious,
slow to anger, abounding in love. ... For as high as the heavens are above
the earth, so great is his love for those who fear him' (Ps 103:8, 11).

We see that love perfected and in all its fullness in the person of Jesus Christ (1 Cor 1:18–25). Jesus described eternal life in terms of knowing God (Jn 17:3). He summarised the whole teaching of the law and prophets as the command to "'Love the Lord your God with all your heart and with all your soul and with all your strength and with all your mind", and, "Love your neighbour as yourself'" (Lk 10:27).

The believer's faith relationship with God, expressed in terms of love and fear, is found elsewhere in the New Testament: 'Then the church throughout Judea, Galilee and Samaria enjoyed a time of peace and was strengthened. Living in the fear of the LORD and encouraged by the Holy Spirit, it increased in numbers' (Acts 9:31).

Notice the beautiful balance in describing the believers' relationship to God. On the one hand, there was their personal experience of the Holy Spirit working in them and among them, strengthening and encouraging them. On the other hand, there remained respect and awe that it was Almighty God at work, not some tame god of their imagining. Certainly, God is our loving Heavenly Father, but the moment we stop being in awe of the God who made the whole earth and gave us life, we become complacent, even presumptuous. When the death of the Son of God – who carried the weight of God's judgement against our sin and took on personal combat with the powers of evil on our behalf – no longer 'causes us to tremble', then we are in a bad way. When we stop being in awe of the greatness of his love for sinful people like us, then we start to get things out of perspective.

There is another element to the link between fear and love in our relationship with God. Think of a child in a loving family, playing in the backyard and totally absorbed in a game. The child chases a ball out into the street, oblivious of the truck coming round the corner. The parents, watching helplessly from the window, do not whisper a gentle loving word in such a situation. No, they shout out, 'Stop!', or scream out the child's name. In this situation, given that the parent does not communicate by shouting at normal times, fear and respect will cause the child to obey. To evoke fear in someone is not necessarily the opposite of love: it can be an expression of love in a dangerous situation.

God warns us because he loves us. He sees better than we do the trouble that will come if we refuse to listen to him.

Love and fear coexist within a covenant relationship. The more we are in awe of the greatness and holiness of God, the more we are amazed that he should love us and call us his children (1 Jn 3:1).

Reflection

1. Think about where you stand with God. Do you fear him in a positive way, respecting his awesome power and authority? Or do you fear him in a negative way, fearing that he may not forgive you?
2. Read some of the wonderful statements God has given us to take away our fear: Romans 8:1, 1 Timothy 1:15–16, 1 John 1:8–9 and 5:13.
3. Read 1 John 4:17–18. How does our love for God, in response to his love for us, drive away fear?

20. FAITHFUL RELATIONSHIPS

Read Proverbs 3:1–4

Do not let loyalty and faithfulness forsake you; bind them around
your neck, write them on the tablet of your heart. So you will find
favour and good repute in the sight of God and of people
(3:3–4, NRSV).

Love and faithfulness are coupled together as highly desirable qualities in
the book of Proverbs. They're desirable because they stand at the core of
strong relationships – in friendships, in the family and in marriage. They're
desirable because when love and faithfulness go out the door, relationships
fall apart and life gets messy.

Sexual temptation

Proverbs contains many earthy pictures of infidelity, notably in chapters
5 and 7. There is the married man, tempted to break his marriage vows
with the attractive young woman whose lips 'drip honey' (5:3). There is
the bored, lonely woman whose husband is away on a business trip (7:19–
20) and the young man cruising the streets in the evening looking for
girls (7:8–9). Playing with sexual sin in any form, warns Proverbs, is like
scooping fire into your lap (6:27): you are likely to get burned. It will surely
end in tears and bitterness (5:4).

Human nature has not changed since the days the Proverbs were
written. Have a look at your local paper and turn to the advertisements,
where you will mostly likely find a directory of females and males offering
a range of sexual services. If you are a business traveller, you will have faced
the temptation of the 'adult' movie channels offered in most hotel rooms.
This is in addition to all the steamy hotlines advertised and the flood of
pornography on the internet.

Proverbs gives us graphic warnings about sexual temptation (5:1–23;
6:20—7:27). This is a word to the travelling businessperson, tired and alone
in their hotel room, or to the one walking the back streets of any of the
world's cities and being enticed into bars and nightclubs of various sorts. It
is a word to those who follow the crowd: 'My son, if sinful men entice you,
do not give in to them' (1:10).

So far as we know, these proverbs were written by men and the warnings
are addressed mainly to fellow males. Clearly, Proverbs directs its fire at

males, but there is much here that we all, men and women, need to heed in order to protect ourselves and our relationships from sexual temptation: don't follow the crowd on a boys' or girls' night out; don't get sucked into the culture of flirting in the office; respect those who are married or in long-term relationships.

This is stuff you probably won't hear in the Sunday sermon at church. But we all know that in modern Western society, sexual temptation does not so much 'lie in wait' for us; it comes up and grabs us by the throat!

Love and faithfulness

The focus in Proverbs is not so much on sexual sin per se, but rather that these foolish actions are a betrayal of the commitment to love and faithfulness that was made to the spouse in the marriage covenant. For those who are single, sexual activity outside of a committed, loving marriage relationship can be a destructive force in our own lives and in the lives of others.

The word used for 'love' in Proverbs 3:3 is *hesed*, a word used frequently in the Old Testament to describe the love of God for his people. So rich in meaning that no single English word can do it full justice, it is variously translated in our English versions of the Bible as 'steadfast love', 'unfailing love', 'devotion', 'mercy', 'loving-kindness' or 'constant love'. It is about God's loyal devotion towards us.

As we seek to live a life consistent with the character of God, love and faithfulness are to characterise our lives and relationships. We are 'to write them on the tablets of our hearts' – that is, to make them central to our lives. We are to 'bind them round our necks', which is to make them a constant reminder of their importance: to keep them 'front of mind', as we might say.

This last image also reminds us that, like jewellery designed to adorn the beauty of the wearer, so love and faithfulness bring beauty to lives and relationships: 'Let love and faithfulness never leave you; bind them around your neck, write them on the tablet of your heart' (3:3).

Reflection

1. Think about the relationships you value most and the covenant commitments you have made. In what practical ways can you show these qualities of love and faithfulness?
2. What does it mean for you, in practical terms, to 'bind them around your neck' and 'write them on the tablet of your heart'? (3:3).

21. RESOLVING CONFLICT

Read Proverbs 15:1–18

A gentle answer turns away wrath, but a harsh word stirs up anger
(15:1).
A hot-tempered person stirs up conflict, but the one who is patient
calms a quarrel (15:18).

All relationships experience times of conflict; the test is how we deal with these times.

In situations where people start expressing strong opinions, when emotions get fired up, then there is often a critical moment of choice for those involved: to escalate the scale of the conflict, or to resolve it. Some people choose to adopt a more conciliatory tone, perhaps offering an apology or starting to speak in more rational terms. In other situations, opinions get hardened, voices get louder, tables get thumped and both sides start saying and doing things they are likely to regret later on. Or people may choose to start playing the victim, positioning themselves such that resolving the conflict is made more difficult.

These two proverbs present us with a clear choice. The gentle answer will turn away anger; the patient person will calm the quarrel. But the hot-tempered person who only has harsh words to offer adds fuel to the flames and stirs up conflict, or as some say, 'opens a can of worms'. One way is wise; the other is foolish. 'It is to one's honour to avoid strife, but every fool is quick to quarrel' (20:3).

Consequential damage

We need to remember that our choice will have consequences.

We cannot control the consequential damage of angry or provocative words; we don't know where they will take us, nor how the argument will end. 'Starting a quarrel is like breaching a dam, so drop the matter before a dispute breaks out' (17:14). We may say things that wound, or cause hatred and resentment. The situation can quickly degenerate into violence: 'The lips of fools bring them strife, and their mouths invite a beating' (18:6). We may even make an enemy for life, just because we felt the need to get things off our chests.

We also need to heed the negative effects of a lack of self-control: 'Like a city whose walls are broken through is a person who lacks self-control'

(25:28). The picture is one of chaos and defenselessness: the person who loses it, who shouts and screams – whether in road rage, office rage or in a drunken brawl – is no longer thinking or controlling what comes out of their mouth. They are certainly not concerned about the effect of those words on the situation, or on anyone else. The person in full flight may feel that they are in control and acting powerfully, but Proverbs gives us the more penetrating picture: they are really out of control and are therefore vulnerable. They are like a city whose walls have been broken through and broken down.

By contrast, self-control is listed in the New Testament as one of the fruits of the Holy Spirit (Gal 5:22). It is the outward evidence of God being at work in our life.

Critical conversations

Managing conflict situations does not mean that we should never rebuke someone we believe to be in the wrong, or avoid saying the hard things that sometimes need to be said. Nor does it mean allowing ourselves to be verbally bullied by people with strong personalities and a way with words. It does mean being willing to apologise and admit when we are wrong.

In one of my former workplaces, we used to speak about a need for a 'critical conversation' when issues were not being resolved and unrest and resentment were bubbling away under the surface.

Wisdom recognises that it is not necessarily *what we say* that creates unnecessary conflict, it is *the way we say it*; our attitude is revealed in our body language and facial expressions. In some cultures, strong robust conversations with loud voices are common. In others, shouting and outward expressions of anger are socially unacceptable and cause great offence. Wisdom will at least recognise the cultural norms before launching into conflict.

It is said that in war, truth is often the first casualty. In personal conflict situations, truth is often replaced by gross exaggeration: 'You *never* help around the house'; 'You are *always* out partying'; 'You *never* listen to me, you *always* want your own way.' This outpouring of lies (14:5) is often accompanied by hurtful and abusive barbs as we vent our anger and lose self-control. At this point, wisdom has gone out the window and we start to damage other people in the desire to express our own hurts and frustrations. In the process, we may also damage a relationship that is precious to us.

'A wronged brother is more unyielding than a fortified city; disputes are like the barred gates of a citadel' (18:19). This is a graphic picture of the kind of warfare into which bad relationships may quickly degenerate. Once you have really hurt or offended someone, the barriers go up, and they are very hard to break down.

No doubt we can all learn from the various conflict-resolution strategies and techniques taught by commuication experts to help us in our friendships, marriages and workplaces. But Proverbs is a wise place to start.

Reflection

1. Think about a conflict situation you have been in recently, at home or at work. How does God want you to resolve it?
2. Think of a conflict situation between others close to you. How can you help resolve that?
3. 'Flee, fight or fudge' (avoid the issue) are the three typical responses to conflict. Which action are you most likely to adopt? Why?

22. GOOD ROLE MODELS

Read Proverbs 31

Charm is deceptive and beauty is fleeting; but a woman who fears the LORD is to be praised. Honour her for all that her hands have done, and let her works bring her praise at the city gate (31:30–31).

It is human nature to want to emulate others, to model ourselves on significant people in our lives. I grew up reading true-story adventure books. My heroes were great explorers and mountaineers: Scott and Shackleton; Muir, Mawson, Amundsen, Tillman and Shipton. They were my role models. Later in life I was inspired by the adventures of pioneer missionaries who exchanged their comfortable lives in Europe and America for service in Africa, China and India: people like David Brainerd, Hudson Taylor, James Fraser, William Carey, Amy Carmichael and Gladys Aylward. I still like to read biographies.

The stories of great men and women can inspire us, but they can also leave us feeling rather inadequate: 'What have I achieved compared to them?' We may feel a little like that after reading the last chapter of Proverbs. 'How can I possibly measure up to that standard?'

Wisdom in person

Alongside providing warning and instruction, the book of Proverbs presents us with role models, putting flesh on the bones of what wisdom looks like in real people. We may not measure up to the standard, but the role models are there to inspire us and to show us the quality of life that results from living out all facets of wisdom that Proverbs presents to us. They are there so that we say to ourselves, 'I want to be like that. I want to live like that.'

The wise and good woman in Proverbs 31 is described in terms of an ideal wife: 'A wife of noble character who can find? She is worth far more than rubies' (31:10). This is a woman who plans, works hard, provides for her household and invests for the future. She is generous and inspires confidence. 'She watches over [that is, manages] the affairs of her household' (31:27). The quality and integrity of her life is recognised in the community (31:31). 'She is clothed with strength and dignity; she can laugh at the time to come' (31:25). Why? Because of her prudent planning and hard work (31:24).

Though this passage is describing a 'wife of noble character' (31:10), most of the qualities attributed to her are not role specific or even gender specific. As Waltke puts it:

> This valiant wife has been canonized as a role model for all Israel for all time. Wise daughters aspire to be like her, wise men seek to marry her (v10), and all wise people aim to incarnate the wisdom she embodies, each in his own sphere of activity. One should avoid emphasizing one of these applications at the expense of another, forgetting that by nature proverbial material sets forth exemplars, asking audiences to make the appropriate application to their own spheres.[23]

This role model's characteristics of wisdom, strong work ethic (31:15, 27), wise planning (31:14, 15), wise commercial dealing (31:16) and generosity to the poor (31:20) are ones that recur throughout Proverbs, and they apply to us all: single or married, female or male.

Faithful relationships

This passage also highlights the quality of the relationships that wisdom brings. For the 'wife of noble character', her relationship with her husband is one of mutual respect, affection and admiration (31:11, 23, 28b), as is her relationship with her children. She provides for them, and they speak out their respect, love and admiration for her (31:28). Underpinning her character, and the quality of her relationships, is the woman's relationship of faith with the LORD, which is more valuable that any aspect of outward appearance: 'Charm is deceptive, and beauty is fleeting; but a woman who fears the LORD is to be praised' (31:30).

This godly woman has attracted a godly man. 'Her husband is respected at the city gate, where he takes his seat among the elders of the land' (31:23). Equally, the godly man is wise enough to value and love and respect his wife. He has full confidence in her.

The role model for a godly man is pictured more fully, earlier in Proverbs, in the words of a father's instruction to his son. The writer describes the life that will follow the one who 'preserves sound judgment and discernment' (3:21): such a man will be able to lie down and go to sleep at night without a burden of fear or worry because his trust is in the LORD (3:24). Like the godly woman, he will be free from anxiety about the future or fear of any sudden disaster. Why? Because the LORD will be his confidence and will keep his foot 'from being snared' (3:26). Like the

---

23 Waltke, *Proverbs*, vol. 2, p. 520.

godly woman, he willbe generous and 'will not withhold good from those to whom it is due' (3:27–28).

As he gets older, the godly man will not only stay faithful to his wife, he will increasingly love and cherish her: 'May you rejoice in the wife of your youth ... may you ever be intoxicated with her love' (5:18–20). He will develop good relationships of trust and honesty with his neighbour (3:29). He does not envy others because he is looking to the LORD for blessing on his life (3:32).

The lives and relationships of the people described in Proverbs are characterised by love, integrity, faithfulness and respect, qualities that spring from their faith in the God who is himself loving, faithful, just and worthy of worship. These qualities also beautify their lives and produce beautiful relationships.

Consider those people who have been good role models for you. Just thinking about them may bring a smile to your face, spurring you on to face life with renewed energy and wisdom and with a commitment to 'grow in the grace and knowledge of our Lord Jesus Christ' (2 Pet 3:18). In the words of Proverbs, 'even their memory is a blessing' (10:7).

Reflection

1. In the context of these role models in the book of Proverbs, read also Psalm 15. What are the qualities of the role model (male or female) described there?
2. Who are your role models? Which of their characteristics do you most admire and wish to emulate?
3. Do you have wise people in your list of role models?

PART TWO

PSALMS:
SONGS FROM THE HEART

A BLESSED LIFE

When life is going well for us, how do we describe it? We might say, 'I have been very *lucky* with the way things turned out when I bought my apartment' or 'I have been very *successful* in my business.' Or, we might say – and this phrase is coming back into common use even in secular society – 'I have been *blessed*.' This term is often used as a way of diverting attention away from the speaker's own merit and achievements and indicating the hand of some unspecified higher power.

In Psalms, to be blessed is to find the true happiness that can only be found in being in right relationship with God. It is possible to experience this true happiness whatever our immediate circumstances, moods or feelings.

Psalms commonly uses two different Hebrew words for 'blessed'. The first one, *ashre*, which occurs 26 times in Psalms, is sometimes translated 'happy' or 'fortunate'. The second, *barak*, is usually translated 'bless'. It appears in Psalms, in different forms, 74 times – for example in 18:46, 28:6, and 31:21 – and occurs some 330 times in the Old Testament.[24] To 'bless' God means that we praise him. When God blesses us, he acts with love and goodness towards us. He may also enable one person to be a blessing to others, as when God promised Abraham that he would be a blessing to the nations (Gen 12:2–3).

As Mowinckel comments: 'To have blessing includes whatever the Israelites meant by the term "Shalom", "wholeness", "welfare", "harmony" or "peace."'[25] It is a striking alternative to the common human experiences of anxiety, fear and doubt.

24 Young et al., *Concordance*, pp. 97–99.
25 Mowinckel, *Psalms*, p. 44.

23. A STATEMENT OF FAITH

Read Psalm 1

Blessed is the one who does not walk in step with the wicked
or stand in the way that sinners take or sit in the company of
mockers, but whose delight is in the law of the LORD, and who
meditates on his law day and night (1:1–2).

The book of Psalms begins with a statement of faith. Psalm 1 first describes
the person who is truly happy, who is blessed by God (1:1–2), then pictures
them as like a healthy fruit tree (1:3) and finally contrasts them with 'the
wicked' (1:4–6).

The description

What does a blessed life look like? What makes truly happy people? The first
two verses give the answer. They do not do what is contrary to the word of
God just because others think it is a good idea or they are pressured to do
so. They do not 'stand in the way that sinners take' by identifying with or
following those whose beliefs and behaviours sink to the lowest common
denominator. And they do not 'sit in the company of mockers' – those who
ridicule faith and all efforts by people of faith to live a godly life. Rather,
they delight in reading and meditating on the word of God and applying
it to their life.

The picture

This happy person is pictured as a growing tree, continually drawing life
from the stream.[26] Such a tree does not die in the burning heat of summer,
because its roots go deep into the water. It is not blown over in the wildest
storm, because its root system is strong.

We lived for six years on the island of Mauritius. Every year we would
experience cyclones, with winds of two- to three-hundred kilometres per
hour, and occasionally some direct hits that inflicted substantial damage.
After a cyclone had passed, we saw huge baobab trees blown over by the
force of the wind. How could such strong-looking trees blow over so easily?
The answer lay in their very shallow root system: the roots did not go deep
and were not strong enough to hold the trees upright in a storm.

---

26 The prophet Jeremiah uses similar imagery for a person whose trust is in the LORD (Jer 17:7).

In this psalm, the tree has firm roots to withstand drought and storm. Its leaves do not wither (1:3): they are always green and healthy and provide beauty and shade. It continues to bear fruit for the enjoyment and nourishment of others.

This is a beautiful picture of the life of someone who delights in the word of God, seeking to live a godly life even when surrounded by 'the wicked', 'the sinners' and 'the mockers'.

The call of Psalm 1 is very simple and direct: make sure you are planted by the water and that your roots go deep! That is, live in close relationship with God. Make the Scriptures your daily study and delight, and don't get tangled up in the evil of this world (Rom 12:1–2). In our *thinking*, we are not to 'walk in step with the wicked'; in our *behaviour*, we are to be different and not to 'stand in the way that sinners take'; and in our *belonging*, we are to ally ourselves with God's people rather than those who ask, rhetorically and derisively, 'where is your God?' (Ps 42:10).

The contrast

Proverbs is full of contrasts, as we have seen, between the wise and foolish, the proud and the humble, those who fear God and those who don't. So the book of Psalms begins by contrasting a tree, which is strong, useful and growing, with the chaff, which is rootless, weightless and useless, easily blown away in the wind (1:4).

This is the contrast between the godly believer and the 'wicked' who *appear* to be people of substance (see also Psalm 73) but actually have none. They have no relationship with the Creator they have rejected, and they leave nothing of value behind (1:5–6).

Roots and growth

Have you ever tried to dig up even a small tree? It is usually very hard work, and it is a big surprise to amateur gardeners like me to discover how far the roots spread out in search of water. A healthy tree grows in two directions at once. Above the ground, there will be visible growth as the trunk enlarges, the branches thicken and spread and as the leaves and fruit grow. But there will also be growth below the ground as the network of roots spreads and deepens, sucking up the life-giving moisture. This is the hidden part.

We are usually much more concerned with what is visible, with what we look like, what people think of us and the image we project. But if we are wise, we give greater attention to the hidden part, to the source of our life and strength. We do this as we stick close to Jesus, keeping the communication channels open: as we pray, listen to God's word and seek to live it out with the strength he gives us.

When we concentrate only on growing the visible part, we're fighting a losing battle because we are trying to live contrary to nature, to the way our Creator designed us.

Let us hold clear in our minds this attractive picture of the tree planted by the water: it is God's purpose for us. Just as the tree is not immune to trouble – frost, heat and drought – so the believer is not immune to sickness, pain and stress. But, as the tree draws life from the water through its root system, so we draw daily strength from God.

Reflection

This statement of faith resoundingly nails the writer's colours to the mast: the godly person is blessed by God. We know that life doesn't always work out quite as simply as envisaged in this psalm. How then would you respond to these questions:

1. Why is it then that good people with no faith, even evil people, often seem to do so well without God? Why do the 'bad guys' often succeed and the 'good guys' suffer problems?
2. What happens when we want to live out this psalm but fail in our attempts to live up to the standard?
3. As we will see in many of the psalms that follow, the writers grapple with both these questions and with other day-to-day practical difficulties, challenges and frequent failures to live out the faith professed in Psalm 1. This psalm pictures our life as a tree planted by a stream. What does it mean in practical terms to put your roots deep into the water?

24. THE BLESSING OF FORGIVENESS

Read Psalm 32

Blessed is the one whose transgressions are forgiven, whose sins
are covered. Blessed is the one whose sin the LORD does not count
against them and in whose spirit is no deceit (32:1–2).

Psalm 1 describes the happy state of the godly person. But what happens
when human sinfulness upsets this idyllic scene and reality bites hard?
What happens when we sin and fail, as all human beings frequently do?

I once played golf with an insurance salesman. He spent the first nine
holes trying to sell me a life insurance policy. We spent the second nine
talking about more personal issues and matters of faith. He confided that
his marriage had failed and, on the last hole, expressed this belief: 'God
could never forgive me – I've broken my promises to my wife.'

David, the writer of Psalm 32, clearly understood this feeling of guilt
and this longing for forgiveness. He had also come to realise the priceless
blessing of being forgiven by God.

Recognising our need for forgiveness

The prerequisite for forgiveness is confession and repentance, but that
comes at a cost to our pride. It is anathema to positive thinkers, who see all
talk of sin as negativity and 'bad karma' and urge us to focus only on the
positives. It is irrelevant to secular atheists, who believe there is no God
and that prayers of repentance are therefore just words floating out into
an empty universe. It is totally contrary to the received wisdom of populist
religion that we are basically good people, albeit with a few shortcomings
and weak points, and that God – if there *is* 'anyone upstairs' – will see that
we are all OK at the end.

David knew the reality. He knew that he had transgressed (32:1); he had
crossed the boundaries and broken God's laws. He also knew that this was
not an occasional lapse from the norm of good behaviour. He had a deeper
problem called 'sin': a cancer eating away at his soul that could not be
healed by superficial treatment. He knew that he was fundamentally a rebel
against the authority of God, and that he had failed to achieve any target
of godliness he had ever aimed at. He expresses, in very emotion-charged
language, the experience of carrying a burden of guilt and unconfessed sin.

When I kept silent, my bones wasted away through my groaning all day long. For day and night your hand was heavy upon me; my strength was sapped as in the heat of summer. Then I acknowledged my sin to you and did not cover up my iniquity. I said, 'I will confess my transgressions to the LORD.' And you forgave the guilt of my sin (32:3–5).

He shares 'the experience of forgiveness and release that came from owning up to sin after attempting to deny it,'[27] and affirms that all who confess their sin to God, and receive his forgiveness, are truly blessed.

Before I came to faith in Christ, I thought of God only in terms of providing an answer to my questions. I wanted to know what was true. When I began to read the Bible, I learned that my self-centeredness was itself the barrier between God and me. But God, in his love, had reached out to me, accepted me and forgiven me. I learned that 'religion' is about human beings searching for God. Christianity is about God searching for us, looking for us like a good shepherd rounding up his lost sheep (Jn 10:11–18; Isa 53:6).

Being sure of God's forgiveness

Like my golfing friend, you may feel that God could never love you or forgive you. You may think it would be foolish and presumptuous to claim any certainty that God had forgiven you. The death of Jesus Christ on the cross tells us that all such feelings are a lie.

The Bible insists that we *can* be sure, not because of our goodness, or the strength of our faith, but because of Jesus Christ and what he has done. To find assurance, we need to look up and out to Jesus Christ, rather than search inwardly for the answers. He died for us, carrying the oppressive weight of our sin and of God's just judgement on sin so that we can be free of guilt and condemnation and be justified in his court. He died for us because he loves us, and because of his death we are forgiven and accepted by God (See Romans 3–5).

There was a period in my life which lasted several months when I doubted whether I was really forgiven. I learned to understand and rely on the logic of the Bible, which goes something like this:

1. I am sinful.
2. All people are sinful (Rom 3:23).
3. Jesus died for sinners (Rom 5:8).
4. Therefore, Jesus died for me.
5. Therefore, I am forgiven and justified in his sight. Thank God!

---

27 Goldingay, *Psalms*, vol. 1, p. 453.

When you realise this, you know, like the psalmist, that you are truly blessed to *have* your sins forgiven and doubly blessed to *know* your sins are forgiven. No wonder this psalm ends on a high note: 'Many are the woes of the wicked, but the LORD's unfailing love surrounds the one who trusts in him. Rejoice in the LORD and be glad, you righteous; sing, all you who are upright in heart' (32:10–11).

The way of life presented in this and many other psalms is one of thankfulness, praise, freedom and the blessing of God. Why, then, would we carry on in anxiety, guilt and fear?

Reflection

1. Read Romans 4. What point is made by the Apostle Paul when he quotes Psalm 32?
2. Read Psalm 103. How does the writer turn the knowledge and experience of God's forgiveness into praise and thanksgiving? (See Ps 103:2, 3, 12.)
3. Read Psalm 67:1–2. What is the flow-on effect of God's blessing on your own life into the lives of others?

25. THE BLESSING OF KNOWING GOD

Read Psalms 40 and 41[28]

Blessed is the one who trusts in the LORD, who does not look to
the proud, to those who turn aside to false gods (40:4).

In Psalm 40, David looked back to how the LORD had helped him and
restored him in a troubled time: 'He lifted me out of the slimy pit, out of the
mud and mire' (40:2); 'He set my feet on a rock'; 'He put a new song in my
mouth' (40:2, 3). In Psalm 41, David remembers again how the LORD had
delivered him in time of trouble (41:1) and preserved his life in the face of
sickness (41:3), sin (41:4) and the hatred of his enemies (41:5, 7, 11a).

Looking back on his experiences, David concludes that being able to
trust in the LORD in the dark times is a great blessing. He realised that his
faith could also be an inspiration to others: 'Many will see and fear the
LORD and put their trust in him' (40:3).

Trusting God

It is one thing to say we believe in God; it is another to actually trust God.
The former may be a purely intellectual belief that makes little difference to
the way we live. The latter is life changing: it affects our attitudes, behaviour
and actions in every part of life. This is the sort of trust celebrated by the
psalmist.

Trusting God is contrasted here with turning aside to, and relying on,
false gods (40:4). In the society in which I live, those 'gods' are typically
fame (celebrity), money, success and self-fulfilment, or some combination
of these. As we go through tough times, and as we demand answers to
our big questions of life and death, all of these false gods will eventually
disappoint, failing to deliver any lasting answers to our questions.

We should understand, however, that the blessing of God is not
necessarily linked with financial success, possessions, great achievements
or even good health. At the beginning of Psalm 40, David recalls and
celebrates God's help in the past. But, perhaps surprisingly, the psalm
doesn't end on a note of triumph. Rather, we find David back down in the
pit, but still trusting God and looking to God for his help: 'But, as for me,
I am poor and needy; may the Lord think of me. You are my help and my
deliverer; you are my God, do not delay' (40:17).

---

28   Refer also to Psalms 65, 84, 94 112, 119 and 128.

One of the marks of true faith is the continuing trust and worship of God when all the cards seem to be stacked against us. The message of Psalms is that there is blessing in the relationship *in itself*, not just because of what God may give us.

Let's flesh out this picture by looking at some other aspects of a blessed and happy life described in Psalms.

Experiencing God's blessing

Psalms shows us a whole range of attitudes and actions that attract the blessing of God. But underlying them all is the privilege of knowing God and experiencing his grace at work in our lives. Here are some of the blessings from God as found in Psalms:

- God's blessing is promised for those who show his love and care for others: 'Blessed are those who have regard for the weak; the LORD delivers them in times of trouble' (41:1).
- God's blessing is promised for those deal fairly with others: 'Blessed are those who act justly, who always do what is right' (106:3).
- God's people are privileged in being called to worship him and experience his presence: 'Blessed are those you choose and bring near to live in your courts' (65:4).
- Those who love and obey God's word are blessed: 'Blessed are those whose ways are blameless, who walk according to the law of the LORD. Blessed are those who keep his statutes and seek him with all their heart' (119:1–2); and 'Blessed are those who fear the LORD, who finds great delight in his commands' (112:1).
- Finding strength in God is a blessing: 'Blessed are those whose help is the God of Jacob, whose hope is in the LORD their God, the Maker of heaven and earth … he remains faithful for ever' (146:5–6).
- Even God's discipline is a blessing: 'Blessed is the one you discipline, LORD, the one you teach from your law' (94:12).

Many of these statements about blessing in Psalms are reminiscent of Proverbs (see, for example, Pss 41:1 and 128:1). There is the same mix of awe and joy, fear and delight in our relationship with God.

We find a similar compatibility of seeming opposites in some human relationships. When I was at school, the favourite schoolteacher was not some kindly old guy who gave us chocolates and let us get away with murder, but a fair but strict disciplinarian who was committed to teaching us and bringing out the best in us. He would break out into a big smile when he saw we had grasped what he was teaching us, and he would be patient with our efforts when he could see we were trying. Almost everyone in his classes raised their performance, because we all sensed that he was there for us and had our best interests at heart. Affection and respect were compatible parts of the relationship he established with his students.

So too in our relationship with God; we find that his instruction and discipline are essential parts of his love for us. He is totally committed to our ultimate good. In the words of one New Testament writer: 'God disciplines us for our good, in order that we may share in his holiness' (Heb 12:10).

Psalms, like Proverbs, sets before us how God wants us to live: enjoying a relationship of faith with him, trusting him and learning to draw on his strength in the face of all difficulties. It is truly a blessed life.

Reflection

1. How have you experienced the blessing of God in your life?
2. Think of the tough times in your life. In what ways has God blessed you through those situations?
3. What blessings are described in these verses in Psalms: 5:12; 10:3; 28:9; 29:11; 45:2; 65:10; 67:1, 6, 7; 107:38; 115:13; 128:5; 134:3; 147:13? Write them down to remind yourself of the blessings that come from your relationship with God.

26. THE BLESSING OF BELONGING TO GOD'S PEOPLE

Read Psalm 100

Know that the LORD is God. It is he who made us, and we are his;
we are his people, the sheep of his pasture (100:3).

Some psalms are individual prayers, communication between a single believer and God. But many others are songs of communal worship. They are about 'we' and 'us', not just 'I' and 'me'. In Psalm 100, we celebrate the truth that God has formed his people and we belong to him; we are *his* people and, like sheep belong to a shepherd, we belong to the LORD our Shepherd (100:3).

We are his people

There is great happiness to be enjoyed in our personal relationship with God. But Psalms recognises that one of the blessings of belonging to God is that we also belong to his people. As Mowinckel comments, 'The basic reality in human life is, for the Israelite, not the individual but the community.'[29] The psalmist puts it even better: 'Blessed is the nation whose God is the LORD, the people he chose for his inheritance' (33:12); and, 'Blessed is the people of whom this is true; blessed is the people whose God is the LORD' (144:15).

We therefore have psalms addressed to other believers, rather than God himself, that invite and encourage fellow believers to praise God: 'Sing joyfully to the LORD, you righteous' (33:1); 'Come and hear, all you who fear God; let me tell you what he has done for me' (66:16).[30]

It's not surprising, therefore, that many psalms were used in corporate worship. They became the people's songbook-cum-prayerbook, collated for use in the rebuilt temple after their return from the Babylonian exile. What might have been surprising to the original authors is the extent to which they have continued to be used in worship, by millions around the world, for well over two millennia.

---

29 Mowinckel, *Psalms*, p. 42.
30 See also Psalms 66 and 81: 'Shout for joy to God, all the earth! Sing the glory of his name' (66:1–2); 'Sing for joy to God our strength' (81:1).

The community of God's people

The New Testament describes this community of faith with several word pictures. We are 'the church of God [the *ecclesia*, the 'called-out community'], which he bought with his own blood' (Acts 20:28); the 'body of Christ', in which each member has a different role (1 Cor 12). We are like a building (Eph 2:19–22; 1 Pet 2:5), with each of us like a living stone, hand-placed by God, the master builder, to form part of the whole. We are (collectively) the bride of Christ (Eph 5:25–27) and we are like branches joined to a vine (Jn 15).

The Christian believer, through the grace of God, therefore also belongs to a new community and can celebrate that God has brought this about. We commonly talk about '*going* to church'; we think in terms of attendance at a place or an event. But the biblical picture is one of *belonging*. When people become Christians, they find that they belong to Christ – and also, therefore, to his people.

My wife and I have lived for extended periods in six different countries. My work has taken me to some twenty more. Wherever we go we find a common bond with Christians, whatever their skin colour, culture or education. In our church in the Middle East, some fifty different nationalities were represented!

Belonging to God's people is one of the great blessings highlighted in the psalms and indeed throughout the Bible: belonging not just to an earthly family or a local tribe, but also to a global family of believers drawn from 'every nation, tribe, people and language' (Rev 7:9).

Fellowship

The Christian faith is to be lived as well as studied and preached. And it is to be lived out, not by individuals in isolation, but within a community of believers, in what the New Testament calls *koinonia*, usually translated as 'fellowship'.

Some of us are gregarious by nature; some of us are loners. Most of us swing between the two depending on our mood. However much of a loner we are, there comes a time when we crave the warmth of human fellowship. Outside of the church, people look for fellowship in all sorts of places: pubs, fitness centres, coffee shops, political and community groups – even street gangs. We were not created to be alone. We cannot have a full experience of love on our own, therefore we cannot have a full experience of God only on our own. It is together with all God's people that we understand how deep and wide is the love of God (Eph 3:18). The New Testament, like the

Old Testament, majors on the communal experience of God's people, the strong message being that we need each other.

Have you ever looked around your church or bible study group and thought, 'What am I doing here? What do I have in common with all these people who are so different from me?' The answer is *Christ*. He draws us to himself, and through that experience we are drawn closer together.

One young married couple recently shared with me their first experience of Christian fellowship, of the sense of belonging to God's people. Wanting to find out more about the Christian faith, they had hesitantly signed up for a course at their local church. They were extremely uncomfortable on the first evening when they found themselves in a group with people very different from themselves. There was a fifty-year-old recovering alcoholic, a single mother with drug problems, another young woman with poor social skills – 'a bunch of crazies' was the way they described them. But over a period of weeks, a strange thing happened. As this group of very different people studied the Bible, and even began to pray together, they grew to genuinely love and care for each other. This was not just a social phenomenon; there was a spiritual dimension. They were being drawn together by Christ and began to experience what the Bible calls the 'fellowship of the Holy Spirit'.

A church where Christian faith is being lived out is a church with strong bonds of fellowship.

Reflection

1. Read Psalm 133. What are your best experiences of communal worship, Christian fellowship and Christian service together with others? What has made those experiences so special and memorable?
2. Read 1 Peter 2:9–10. What does this tell us about the identity and purpose of God's people? What encouragement do you find here?
3. Have you committed yourself to a local church? If not, why not?

UNDERSTANDING

If you want to understand more about God, read Psalms.

The psalms are revealing. They bring us timeless truth about the character of God so that we might understand and respond in worship. It is not so much that they reveal 'new' truth, things about God not found elsewhere in the Bible, but rather that they turn the truth about God, revealed in the Law and the Prophets, into the language of celebration, worship and prayer.

The result is that truth is *experienced* as well as *understood*. It enters the heart, the core of our being, as well as the head.

Psalms also reveals human nature to us. Its writers lay bare the nature of humankind in all its frailty, but also in all its dignity in being made in the image of God. To make sense of life, we need to understand ourselves. We also need to recognise the fragility and brevity of life, and to face the reality of our own mortality.

Psalms helps us to grow in understanding ourselves, our world and, above all, our Creator.

27. UNDERSTANDING THROUGH THE WORD OF GOD

Read Psalms 19 and 119

The heavens declare the glory of God; the skies proclaim the work
of his hands (19:1).
The law of the LORD is perfect, refreshing the soul (19:7).

God's law and God's word

God has spoken to humankind. That truth is not debated in Psalms; it is accepted and celebrated. God has spoken in creation. He has also spoken to us in the Law (Torah), Prophets and Writings, which together make up our Old Testament. He has spoken supremely in the person of Jesus Christ (Heb 1:1–3) and through his appointed apostles and prophets in the New Testament Scriptures.

For the psalmists, writing in the first millennium before Christ, their 'Bible' was mainly the Torah, the first five books of our Old Testament containing the accounts of creation, God's calling of Abraham, the formation of God's people and their great deliverance from slavery in Egypt – much more than what we would recognise as 'laws'. So, in the Psalms, 'your law' and 'your word' are sometimes interchangeable terms (e.g. 119:28–29).

The psalmist exclaimed, 'Oh, how I love your law!'(119:97). We who have the great privilege of having the whole Bible, not just the Torah, can say with the psalmist, 'Oh, how I love your word!': 'Your word, LORD, is eternal; it stands firm in the heavens' (119:89).

Encountering God

Psalm 19 brings together in one song the truths that God has spoken in his creation (19:1) and his word (19:7). Bible reading is not a matter of religious observance for the psalmist, nor a duty or a chore, but a daily delight. It is 'sweeter than honey' and 'more precious than gold' (19:10). Why? Because as he reads, he expects that God will speak to him. He expects to encounter God through his word.

Five different words are used in this psalm to describe God's verbal communication with us: the law, the statutes, the precepts, the commands and the decrees. Each one is described and assigned a function in the life of the reader (19:7–9):

- The law of the LORD is perfect, refreshing the soul.
- The statutes of the LORD are trustworthy, making wise the simple.
- The precepts of the LORD are right, giving joy to the heart.
- The commands of the LORD are radiant, giving light to the eyes.
- The decrees of the LORD are firm, and all of them are righteous.

The purpose of the God-given law is *good*. God's word is perfect, trustworthy, right, radiant and firm because it expresses the character of God. It is given to reveal God to us.

The effect on the reader is also intended to be positive. The law is given to refresh the soul, make us wise and bring joy to the heart and light to the eyes.

As we read these words with the New Testament in our hands, we know that the law of God also convicts us of our sin and points us to Christ. Only Jesus Christ has ever kept the law, and it is only through his atoning death that the righteous requirements of the law were fulfilled so that we are justified (put right with God) and forgiven (Rom 8:3–4; 5:1). The law of God reveals the character of God to us. It is also intended to show us our need of a Saviour and lead us to Christ (Gal 3:24).

In Psalm 119, the 'magnum opus' of all the psalms, we find a sustained song of praise to the word of God, extolling its purpose and its effects. Like Psalm 19, it uses several different words to help us understand the many different facets of the word of God in this psalm. There are the law (*torah*, 119:1), statutes (*huqqim*, 119:2) and precepts (*piqqudim*, 119:4, meaning particular detailed instructions). There are also the commands (*miswot*, 119:6), decrees (*mispatim*, 119:8), and more general terms such as word (*dabar*, 119:16) and promise (*imra*).[31]

With due apology to any lawyers or historians who may read this, the thought of ploughing through ancient documents dating back over three millennia is not one that would excite most of us. But because it is the word of God, the psalmist finds it both satisfying and illuminating: 'How sweet are your words to my taste, sweeter than honey to my mouth!' (119:103).

Reading the Bible: a chore or a delight?

Reading the Scriptures is not always the joyful experience described in this psalm. Sometimes our eyes skim over the words without taking anything in. Sometimes our minds are dull or distracted, our hearts are cold and our spirits feel lifeless. What then? Do we put our Bible back on the shelf and wait until we are in a better mood, 'in a better place' spiritually? No!

---

31 Kidner, *Psalms*, vol. 2, pp. 417–19.

We need to read, because God wants to say something to us.

Do you find it strange that you can often find many reasons to read anything *but* the Bible? It's actually not so strange, because there is spiritual battle going on. It is not just about busyness or our human sinfulness and weakness: Satan is always out to divert our attention away from the word of God and make us doubt its value and truth (Gen 3:1).

When I go through dry times, I deliberately vary my routine. If I have been using Bible study notes or a commentary, I will put it aside and just read the Scriptures. If I have been reading through a particular book of the Bible, I may instead focus in on one small passage, or even one verse, and make this my meditation for the day.

As we read, let us pray, 'Open my eyes that I may see wonderful things in your law' (119:18) – and then turn it into prayer and praise.

Reflection

1. If your study of the Bible has become dry, ask God to give you a greater hunger to read and hear and study his word. Make a commitment to reading a portion of the Bible each day.
2. Whatever Bible study method you use, it's often helpful to ask yourself some questions as you read:
   - What do I learn about God in this verse and passage?
   - What did this mean to the original hearers?
   - What does it mean for me in the twenty-first century?
   - How can I respond with practical action?

   Ask yourself these questions while reading Psalm 19.

28. UNDERSTANDING THE GREATNESS OF GOD

Read Psalms 90 and 96

Great is the LORD and most worthy of praise; he is to be feared
above all gods. For all the gods of the nations are idols, but the
LORD made the heavens (96:5).

One of the most commonly believed myths in Western popular culture
is that the answers to all the problems we face in this life are to be found
within ourselves: that our destiny is in our own hands and the only strength
available to deal with life lies within.

This philosophy often pervades Christian thinking. Our attention can
shift gradually, even imperceptibly, from God to ourselves. Psalms provides
a wonderful antidote to this way of thinking by revealing to us the God
who is the Creator, King and Judge, the Mighty One, the Holy One who
is everlasting and eternal. Fixing our eyes on God and his attributes, and
offering him our praise and worship, is a sure way to bring our lives into
perspective.

He is the Creator

'In the beginning God created the heavens and the earth' (Gen 1:1).

This, the first and most basic truth about God revealed in the Bible, is
celebrated in many of the psalms. We may stand in awe of the creation, the
power of the sea, the mountains, the wind and the expanse of the universe.
Why then aren't we in greater awe of the Creator? As Psalm 95 says: 'The
sea is his, for he made it, and his hands formed the dry land' (95:5).

The earth is the LORD's (24:1). We are given the privilege of living here
for a while. We may claim ownership to parts of it, but, in time, we return
to the ground from which we were formed. We cannot take even one small
piece of it with us into the afterlife, no matter how many legal documents
of land title we keep in the safe.

When I was a little younger (and fitter), I used to enjoy rock climbing.
One autumn morning, I found myself with a friend walking through the
beautiful Cwm Idwal in North Wales to climb the Devil's Kitchen, a steep
and gloomy cliff in Snowdonia National Park. It was raining, there was
no-one else about, and the rock was unrelentingly sheer and dripping
with water and mud. I am not normally given to fanciful thoughts, but

I started to feel an unusual sense of foreboding, way beyond the normal pre-climbing nerves. What was I doing in the *Devil's* kitchen? Was I asking for trouble? I was seriously thinking about turning back when a verse from Psalm 24 came into mind: *The earth is the LORD's!* We went on to enjoy the day.

We may give names to landscape features such as 'Hell's Gates', 'the throat of the devil' (Iguazu Falls) or the 'Devil's Kitchen', but really, the earth belongs to God. As Abraham Kuyper, the Dutch theologian, commented, 'There is not a single square inch in the whole domain of our human existence over which Christ, who is Sovereign over all, does not cry: "Mine."'[32]

He is the great King

'The LORD reigns, he is robed in majesty' (93:1).

The nation of Israel knew what it was like to have bad kings rule over them. Occasionally they had a good one like Hezekiah or Asa, but mostly they were flawed leaders who failed in the role entrusted to them. The people looked forward to the day when, as the prophets foretold, the great King (the Messiah) would come to rule with justice and bring everlasting peace; one who would be a descendent of David, and yet also divine (2:7–9; 110:1).

In the meantime, the people celebrated the fact that God was himself the great King: not a constitutional monarch of modern Western democracies, but one with absolute power over all the earth. All the earthly kings of Israel were but pale imitations.

God is king, not just of Israel, but over all the earth: 'Ascribe to the LORD, all you families of nations, ascribe to the LORD glory and strength' (96:7); 'Shout for joy to God, all the earth! Sing the glory of his name' (66:1); 'Praise our God, all peoples, let the sound of his praise be heard' (66:8). Therefore, we all owe him worship and honour.

He is the Judge of all

Psalms speaks about God as judge, not so much as someone to be feared but as one who sweeps the world of evil and set injustices to rights. He will not be like corrupt judges who accept bribes, or even like the best of human judges who have limited wisdom and understanding, but 'he will judge the world in righteousness and the peoples with equity' (98:9).

---

32   Bratt, *Abraham Kuyper*, p. 448.

The psalms understand that man's injustice and sinfulness have put the whole creation 'out of kilter'. Things on this earth are not right. Our lives are not right. Relationships are not right, and there is inequality, injustice and pollution of the environment everywhere. When God comes, the very creation will therefore welcome him with song:

> Let the heavens rejoice, let the earth be glad; let the sea resound and
> all that is in it. Let the fields be jubilant, and everything in them; let
> all the trees of the forest sing for joy. Let all creation rejoice before
> the LORD, for he comes, he comes to judge the earth (96:11–13).

We need to get our lives right with God to be ready for his coming.

He is everlasting and eternal

When one of my daughters was little, she picked up my telescope and pointed it towards me, but she was looking through the wrong end. 'Daddy, you look very small and far away,' was her comment.

As adults, when our problems and agendas start to dominate our lives, then God can seem to us 'very small and far away'. As we read the Scriptures, and perhaps especially these great psalms, it's like getting the telescope the right way around. We start to see more clearly how great God is, and in that context we start to get our problems in proportion.

'Before the mountains were born or you brought forth the earth and the world, from everlasting to everlasting you are God' (90:2).

Reflection

1. Psalms reveals to us how great God is: the Creator, the King, the Judge of all, everlasting and eternal. Think about each of these facets of the character of God revealed in Psalms. In what ways has understanding more about God changed the way you think and work and live?
2. In what ways does understanding more about God affect your relationships with other people?
3. What other attributes of God do you find in Psalms? See, for example, Psalm 50 and Psalm 24.

29. UNDERSTANDING GOD IN HUMAN TERMS

Read Psalms 8 and 33

When I look at your heavens, the work of your fingers, the moon
and the stars that you have established; what are human being that
you are mindful of them, mortals that you care for them?
(8:3–4, NRSV).

'I don't think of God as a person. I see him as the spirit of the universe, the "ground of our being."[33] This is how a friend of mine expressed his beliefs after rejecting Christian belief in a personal God.

But God is not inanimate. He is the true and living God. He reveals himself in the Bible as one God in three persons: Father, Son and Holy Spirit. He is the living one who speaks, works, saves, loves, rescues, rules and judges. God has given the human writers several pictures of himself using human physiological terms to aid understanding of his character and his actions. Many psalms make full use of this imagery, speaking of the eyes and ears of God, the face of God, the hand of God, the fingers of God and the arm of God. As we study this imagery, so we come to understand more of God and how he wants to relate to us.

The eyes and ears of the LORD

The truth that God sees us, and sees all that we think and do, may be an unwelcome and even frightening thought if we are trying to hide from him. We have grown used to being monitored in our movements through CCTV, our buying patterns through the internet and our personalities through social networks. But we naturally recoil from the idea that 'big brother is watching us', as described by George Orwell in his novel, *1984*.

Yet in Psalms, as in the rest of the Bible, the truth that God is *El Roi*, 'the one who sees us' (Gen 16:13), is a positive and encouraging reminder of God's providential care for us. 'The eyes of the LORD are on those who fear him, on those who hope in his unfailing love, to deliver them from death and keep them alive in famine' (33:19).

Psalms also speaks about the ears of God, conveying the truth that God not only sees us, he also hears our prayers and answers according to his

---

33 Following Paul Tillich's worldview of 'religious naturalism'.

sovereign will. 'The eyes of the LORD are on the righteous, and his ears are attentive to their cry' (34:15).

The face of God

The light of God's face is an outward display of his good favour. It is the 'smile' of God on our lives: 'Many, LORD, are asking, "Who will bring us prosperity?" Let the light of your face shine upon us' (4:6); 'It was not by their sword that they won the land, nor did their arm bring them victory; it was your right hand, your arm, and the light of your face, for you loved them' (44:3).

It is a beautiful thing to look into the face of another human being that you love – spouse, friend or family member – and to realise how much you care for them and to see in their face their love for you. This sort of intimate, deep moment is envisaged when the psalmist writes about the light of God's face. It is reminiscent of the wonderful Aaronic blessing: 'The LORD bless you and keep you; the LORD make his face shine on you and be gracious to you; the LORD turn his face towards you and give you peace' (Num 6:24–26).

The hand of God and the arm of God

We use our hands to make things, greet people, write and type, show love, play sport and games, and convey messages through gestures and by signs to those who are deaf. We also use them to fight. When we hold things in our hands, we are demonstrating ownership and providing security. In Psalms, we see 'the hand of God' being used in similar ways. The table on the following page lists some of the references.

The arm of the LORD symbolises God's strength in action. 'With your mighty arm you redeemed your people' and 'his right hand and his holy arm have worked salvation for him' (98.1). God's 'hand' is strong (89:13), but when the psalmists want to emphasise this strength, they speak of God's arm also: a picture perhaps of God 'rolling up his sleeves' to get to work, defeating evil and delivering his people.

We sometimes find it hard to believe that God loves us, or to imagine why he ever could love us or even be interested in us. But God is revealed to us in the Bible in terms that we can readily understand, as one whose eyes are always upon us, who hears our prayers, whose face is always turned towards us, who made us with his own hands and who reaches out a hand to rescue us and hold us firm.

The hand of God in Psalms

God's action	Text in psalms	Reference
Creating the world	'His hands formed the dry land'	95:5
Creating human life	'Your hands made me and formed me'	119:73
In his power and control	'My times are in your hands'	31:15
In correction and discipline	'Your hand was heavy on me'	32:4
Providing eternal security	'Into your hands I commit my spirit'	31:5
Providing present security	'My times are in your hands'	31:15
Showing compassion	'Lift up your hand O God. Do not forget the helpless'	10:12
Acting strongly to save	'By your hand save me'	17:14
Performing mighty acts	'They have no regard for the deeds of the LORD and what his hands have done';	28:5
	'With your hand you drove out the nations'	44:2
Acting in power	'Your arm is endowed with power; your hand is strong, your right hand exalted'	89:13
Keeping us from disaster	'The LORD upholds him with his hand'	37:24
Exercising judgment	'In the hand of the LORD is a cup [of judgment]'	75:8
Providing for our needs	'When you open your hand, they are satisfied with good things'	104:28
Acting in love to help	'Save me in according to your unfailing love. Let them know that it is your hand, that you, LORD, have done it';	109:27
	'May your hand be ready to help me';	119:173
	'Reach down your hand from on high; deliver me and rescue me from the mighty waters'	144:7
Showing his character by his actions	'The works of his hands are faithful and just'	111:7
Defeating our enemies	'You stretch out your hand against the anger of my foes'	138:7
Protecting and guiding	'Your hand will guide me, your right hand will hold me fast'	139:10

Providing for all creation	*'You open your hand and satisfy the desires of every living thing'*	145:16
Supporting and strengthening	*'The LORD upholds him with his hand'*	37:24
Personal blessing	*'You lay your hand upon me'*	139:5

Note: 'The hand of God' is used extensively elsewhere in the Bible. For example, in the context of guidance: 'For the LORD brought you out of Egypt with his mighty hand' (Exod 13:9); and to reassure us of God's love for us: 'My sheep listen to my voice … no one will snatch them out of my hand' (Jn 10:27–28).

Reflection

1. Think about the following statements in Psalms about the hand of God, the eyes of God and the ears of God. In what ways do they strengthen your faith?
2. What does it means to seek the face of God? (2 Chron 7:14).
3. Thank God for his personal love for you.

30. UNDERSTANDING OURSELVES

Read Psalm 139

You have searched me, LORD, and you know me (139:1).

Because we are God's creatures, we can only understand ourselves properly in relation to God. We cannot assess ourselves in isolation from that basic reality. Unlike twenty-first-century Western psychology, the Bible has no categories for considering humankind outside of a relationship with the God who created us.

As John Calvin wisely noted, some six hundred years ago:

> Nearly all the wisdom we possess, that is to say true and sound wisdom, consists of two parts: the knowledge of God and of ourselves … it is certain that man never achieves a clear knowledge of himself unless he has first looked upon God's face, and then descends from contemplating him to scrutinizing himself.[34]

We are known by God

A colleague whose Christian mother had contracted Alzheimer's said this to me: 'She doesn't know who I am. I don't think she knows any longer who Jesus is. But he sure knows who she is!' In the pain of seeing his mother in this condition, he found great reassurance in the knowledge that she is known and kept by God.

God knows all about our physical, mental and spiritual conditions. He knows what we do and even what we think (139:2). He knows where we go and what we are about to say even before we say it. He knows every thought, word, action and motive, and his knowledge of us is complete.

How do we react to that? Perhaps in the same way as the psalmist, with wonder and amazement that God should know us better than we know ourselves. 'Where can I go from your Spirit? Where can I flee from your presence?'(139:7). Or perhaps we resent this invasion of our privacy, and we want to run and hide.

Ever since the Garden of Eden, human beings have tried unsuccessfully to hide from God. We can't do it, though we may try to pretend we can. I used to play hide and seek with my children when they were very young. They would hide in an obviously visible place, such as under the table, but they would place their hands over their eyes so that they couldn't see me

---

34 Calvin, *Institutes of the Christian Religion*, 1.1.2, pp. 35–37.

looking for them. In their perception, at that age, this was the same as me not being able to see them. It seems that, as adults, we try to do the same with God. We put our hands over our eyes and deny he exists and convince ourselves that there is no-one watching what we do, no-one looking for us and calling us to account.

The gospel calls us to come out into the open with God. It is a wonderful relief to give up the pretence and face reality. We then find that God is not seeking us to condemn us, but to save us.

God is to be found everywhere

The traditional African American spiritual asks the question, 'O sinner-man where you gonna run to, all on that day?' Where indeed? Psalm 139 accepts with joy, not fear, that we cannot hide from God, even in the dark, even by moving overseas and making a new start in a different place. When we move in the hope of leaving our problems behind, reality still catches up and we discover that we have taken our biggest problem with us: ourselves. We need to find God – or rather, be found by him.

I first came to faith in Christ in my twenties while in Tanzania. In the course of travelling with my work, I have since met many people who, like me, have become Christians while working away from home, outside their comfort zones, where the familiar props on which they have relied have been removed, prompting them to ask some big questions about themselves and about God.

We were created by God

We are not the chance result of a random combination of chemicals and physical forces; we are God's creations. 'You created my inmost being; you knit me together in my mother's womb' (139:13).

Human beings are not highly developed animals, but creatures made in the image of God. When we forget or deny this, we become sub-human, not more human. It's not surprising, then, that we either develop an inflated view of our own significance – 'I can manage fine without God' – or, at the other end of the spectrum, have problems of self-esteem because we cannot understand how we can be of any value to God.

The psalmist reflects with amazement on the truth that 'all the days ordained for me were written in your book before one of them came to be' (139:16). When we write things down in books, it is usually with a careful, planned intention. The message here is that our loving Creator has carefully and intentionally given us a life he wants us to live. When we grasp this truth, like the psalmist, we want to praise him and worship him: 'I praise you because I am fearfully and wonderfully made' (139:14).

We are sinful

After reflecting on the greatness of God and the miracle of human life, the writer looks around at the world, with its greed, cruelty and injustice. He gets angry at the way the world is and the way evil people seem to prosper. But then he starts to recognise the problem of evil in his own heart, and he ends on a note of sober realism: 'Search me, God, and know my heart; test me and know my anxious thoughts. See if there is any offensive way in me, and lead me in the way everlasting' (139:23–24).

How can we understand ourselves? Who can unravel the complex web of our thoughts, motives and instincts? Who can really explain how we are wired? We can find great relief and peace in knowing that there is a God who made us, who loves us and wants to know him. This personal love of God comes out in this psalm, almost in passing: 'If I rise on the wings of the dawn, if I settle on the far side of the sea, even there your hand will guide me, your right hand will hold me fast' (139:9).

To understand ourselves, let's look to the God who understands us.

Reflection

1. What have you learned in your life so far about yourself? Your strengths and weaknesses? Your motives and values?
2. As you read Psalm 139, ask yourself what it means for you to know that
   - you are made by God
   - you are known by God
   - you are loved by God.

31. UNDERSTANDING THE FRAGILITY AND BREVITY OF LIFE

Read Psalms 90 and 144

They are like a breath; their days are like a fleeting shadow (144:4).

My daughter's third child was born seven weeks premature. When we visited her in the intensive care unit, I was amazed to see tiny newborns of twenty-four and twenty-six weeks' gestation. For one who doesn't spend much time in hospitals, it was a reminder of how precious and fragile is human life, how small the margin between life and death.

However long we live, death is certain in the end. Life passes by all too quickly; that much we know. Even with the best diet, healthcare and exercise programs, we will not go on indefinitely.

Life is short

Yet this isn't a cause for despair or depression in Psalms. Why not? Because the shortness and uncertainty of human life is contrasted with the eternal, faithful, covenant love of God. Our relationship with him goes on beyond death.

In Psalm 90, the shortness of life is likened to a new shoot of grass, which in a hot climate is dried up and dead by evening: 'You sweep people away in the sleep of death – they are like the new grass of the morning: In the morning it springs up new, but by evening it is dry and withered' (90:5–6).

This psalm expresses with poignancy the brevity of our lives. 'Our days may come to seventy years, or eighty, if our strength endures; yet the best of them are but trouble and sorrow, for they quickly pass, and we fly away' (90:10).

But this transience and impermanence is contrasted with God being our eternal home: 'LORD, you have been our dwelling-place throughout all generations ... from everlasting to everlasting you are God' (90:1–2).

It is in this context of recognising our limited and uncertain life spans that we have the prayer: 'Teach us to number our days, that we may gain a heart of wisdom' (90:12). The wise person knows that life is short and takes the opportunity not just to 'live life to the full', but also to be reconciled to God on the way.

'Show me, O LORD, my life's end and the number of my days: let me know how fleeting my life is. You have made my days a mere handbreadth: the span of my years is as nothing before you. Everyone is but a breath, even those who seem secure, a mere phantom' (39:4–6).

These reflections by the psalmist are very reminiscent of those in Ecclesiastes, which, like all the wisdom literature, reminds us that no sense can be made of life or death without reference to God. We can only find significance in our work, our ethics, our relationships and our leisure through a relationship with God.

Preparing for death

A Court Jester was once called to the bedside of the King to beguile his sadness. The jester's mirth, however, failed for once. His best quips drew no corresponding smile from the king's pallid face. 'Master', said the jester, 'why so sad?' 'Because', replied the king, 'I have to leave my home and people and go on a journey.' 'Is it a long journey?' asked the jester. 'It is indeed; the longest journey any man could take.' 'When are you going?' inquired the clown. 'I don't know for certain, but I think it will be quite soon, now.' 'But what of your majesty's preparations?' continued the jester. 'I see no clothing laid out, no boxes in the hall, no horses in the courtyard.' 'Alas!' was the reply, 'You speak the truth. I have had so much else to occupy me that I have made no preparations for departure.' 'Then take my cap and bells', said the bold jester. 'I thought I was the court fool, but I see there lies here a greater fool than I, since he is going on the longest journey man ever took, and yet he calls me here to beguile his precious moments with jest and tale, instead of preparing for his travels.'[35]

Why do we not want to prepare for death or even talk about it? It is the ultimate reality. We try to fill our lives with activity, designed to help us forget our own mortality. Yet every day the news reminds us of people who have died in wars, murders and car accidents, and from disease or old age.

Death is shattering even when we expect it. A friend of our family recently lost her husband, who had battled for two years with acute Alzheimer's disease. Even after being separated from him while he was in hospitals and various nursing homes, she was still not prepared for the awful sense of loss when her husband finally died.

We need to prepare for our own deaths, even if we can never adequately prepare for the loss of a loved one.

---

35 Autton, *Peace at the Last*, preliminary pages.

Reflection

1. Given that life is short and uncertain, what does it mean to live wisely? 'Remember how fleeting is my life. For what futility you have created all humanity! Who can live and not see death, or who can escape the power of the grave?' (89:47–48).
2. How can we prepare to die?
3. How can we overcome fear of death? (see Jn 14:1–6; Heb 2:14–15).

WORSHIP

The psalms are obviously an aid to worship; they have been used in worship for nearly three thousand years. They are still widely used, either in their current forms or adapted by each successive generation into hymns and songs in a musical style that appeals at that time. They are also frequently ransacked by Christian (and even secular) songwriters for phrases, ideas and imagery.

The psalms also reveal to us a great deal *about* worship. Worship frequently involves singing (98:1), music with a whole range of instruments (98:5, 6, 150) and even shouts of joy. It includes praising God and thanking God for who he is and what he has done. It includes reverence for God, prayer and listening to God's word (95). It may also include testimony (66:1), professions of faith and communal statements about the greatness, love and mercy of God (118).

But worship in Psalms, as in all Scripture, is much more than outward form and ceremony. It requires the devotion of our hearts. Jesus quoted the prophet Isaiah in speaking about the religious hypocrites of his day: 'These people honour me with their lips, but their hearts are from me. They worship me in vain' (Mt 15:8–9).

Worship of God means much more than giving him an hour or two each week. It involves our whole lives (Rom 12:1–2; Col 3:17, 23). It is not about 'tacking on' some religious activity to our secular lives, but about embracing a better way to live – God's way.

32. WORSHIPPING GOD

Read Psalm 95

Come, let us bow down in worship, let us kneel before the LORD
our Maker (95:6).

The three R's of education have been characterised as 'reading, 'riting and
'rithmetic'! The three R's of worship revealed to us in Psalm 95 are rejoicing,
reverence and response.

Some churches major on joyful singing, others on a hushed reverence
and others on preaching the word of God and calling for response. True
worship involves all three.

Right from the earliest days of the Christian church, this psalm has
been used as a call and guide to worship. Like many of the psalms, it is
itself a song of worship, but it also tells us a great deal about what worship
involves.

Rejoicing

There are times when we come into God's presence in silence, or in tears,
but it is the great privilege of the believer to come rejoicing: 'Come let us
sing for joy to the LORD; let us shout aloud to the Rock of our salvation.
Let us come before him with thanksgiving and extol him with music and
song' (95:1–2).

The 'shout aloud' is one of homage to the LORD as the great King – the
sort of shout or communal roar we usually reserve for rock stars when they
hit the stage, or for our sporting heroes in their moments of triumph.

To come 'before him' is literally to come before his face, to consciously
enter into his presence with thanksgiving. We have much to be thankful
for, because the God we worship is 'the Rock of our salvation', our Saviour
and deliverer when we are in need.

When we are joyful, we want to sing. Here we sing with joy to the LORD
because he is 'the great God, the great King above all gods' (95:3). In any
human organisation, it's always good to know who is running the show,
who is really in charge. So as we look around this vast amazing universe,
the truth that there is one God, the Creator, who is ultimately in charge, is
a source of great relief and of great joy.

Israel's neighbouring tribes had separate gods for the mountains, plains
and valleys, and others for the sea. These people groups had to be careful

as they moved from one area to another, as they needed to keep the local gods happy. In my early twenties, I worked as a part-time instructor at an outdoor pursuits centre at the foot of Mount Kilimanjaro in Kenya. The climax of the month-long course was an ascent of the mountain, a five-day round trip. We led a group of fifteen African teenagers to the summit. On the way down, a young man from a village in Uganda confided in me that his family back home would never believe he had been to the summit. Why not? Because the belief among his people was that that the spirits who inhabited the mountain would not allow anyone to reach the summit and live to tell the tale.

What a contrast is the God worshipped in this psalm: one who is in control over the mountains, the valleys, the sea and the dry land – the whole lot. We worship an awesome God, and we can rejoice in his true greatness.

Reverence

Rejoicing is the way God invites us to come into his presence, but the key element of worship is reverence for God.

The Hebrew word for worship, used some 170 in the Old Testament, is *shachach*, meaning 'to bow down'. It is used in 1 Samuel 24, when David bows before Saul, and in Ruth 2:10, when Ruth bows low before Boaz. It means, simply, to acknowledge publicly that the one to whom one bows is far greater than oneself.

In the New Testament, the Greek word *proskuneo* is used. It means 'to draw near to kiss': a picture of someone kissing not the cheek or the mouth, but the feet of someone much greater.

In our democratic society, we don't like the idea of bowing down to anyone. But let us at least recognise that if there is a God who created the mountains and the seas and the whole universe, then we owe him our worship. God is great, and therefore we humble ourselves before him.

When God confronts people in the Scriptures, they don't stand around with hands in pockets or lie back on the sofa: they are down on their knees, and often down on their faces, in awe. But whether we worship sitting, kneeling or standing, with hands raised or down at our sides, the Bible reminds us that it is not the body position that is ultimately important in worship. Rather it is the attitude of our hearts: do we really mean it?

Psalm 95 calls us to *rejoice* because of God's greatness and to *reverence* him because of his mercy. Logically, we might want to turn this the other way round. But knowing that God is ultimately in control is a cause for joy, and we reverence him for his mercy because we dare not take that for granted, particularly when we remember what our salvation cost the Son of God.

Response

The third element of worship is our response to the word of God. The tone of Psalm 95 changes abruptly in verse 8 with the warning that we should not shut our ears to what he is saying to us. This psalm looks back to two events during the wilderness wanderings of the children of Israel, before they entered the promised land: at Meribah, they disputed with God, and at Massah, they tested God. They wouldn't believe and they wouldn't obey, so God told them that they would never get to see the land he had given them. They would not 'enter his rest'.

Rejoicing, reverence and response: these are the essentials of worship. And not just on Sundays, but each day: rejoicing in the sovereignty of God, reverencing and respecting him for his mercy and responding to his word.

Reflection

1. Read Amos 5:21–37. Why did the prophet say that the people's worship was not acceptable to God?
2. Think about your experience of public worship. To what extent is it characterised by joy, reverence and listening to the word of God? Reflect on your own approach to worship. What needs to change?
3. Read Romans 12:1–2. Ask God for help to live your whole life as an act of worship.

33. PRAISING AND BLESSING GOD

Read Psalm 103

Praise the LORD, my soul: all my inmost being, praise his holy name.
Praise the LORD, my soul, and forget not all his benefits (103:1–2).

Have you ever come into a worship service with such a heavy heart or a distracted mind that you can barely mouth the words of the songs, let alone sing them from the heart?

I know I have.

We read words like those that begin this psalm – 'Praise the LORD, my soul' – and we shudder, because we don't feel at all like praising and the last thing we want to do is sing. We're too distracted by work worries, money problems and difficult relationships. But worship is a spiritual activity. As we start to praise God, a strange thing often happens. As we think about the truths of the words, and as we join with others in worship, our hearts are gradually warmed by the Spirit of God. We start to worship from the heart.

The psalms are very realistic about this experience. The would-be worshipper prays: 'Open my lips, Lord, and my mouth will declare your praise' (51:15). As God answers that prayer, he enables us to put on 'a garment of praise instead of a spirit of despair' (Isa 61:3).

Remembering his goodness

When our minds are elsewhere and our spirits are dull, Psalms can prompt us to praise God, to deliberately turn our focus away from ourselves and onto him. We are encouraged to 'forget not all his benefits', remember his goodness to us and to call to mind all that he has done.

Psalm 103 helps jog our memories. God has forgiven our sins and healed our diseases (103:3). He has redeemed our lives 'from the pit' and 'crowned us with love and compassion' (103:4). He has never stopped loving, forgiving, strengthening and encouraging us. He has provided for us, and he works by His Holy Spirit to lift and renew our spirits when we are worn out (103:5).

Then, as if remembering again the sinfulness, selfishness and stubbornness of humankind, the psalmist celebrates the wonderful compassion of God who does not treat us as our sins deserve and whose love is greater than we can ever imagine: 'For as high as the heavens are above the earth, so great is his love to those who fear him' (103:11). Does God keep a record of our wrongdoings and failings? No! 'As far as the east is from the west, so far has he removed our transgressions from us' (103:12).

Is that enough to get us praising God? Psalm 103 has much more!

What is God like?

Like many of the psalms, we are encouraged to praise God – not just for what he has done, but for who he is.

He is a God of justice who cares for the oppressed and disadvantaged of this world (103:6), and he therefore calls for us to do the same. We may get angry and concerned about the injustices in this world, but that very sense of injustice comes from God.

He is a God who has spoken and revealed himself to us that we might know him (103:7).

He is a loving Father who cares about his children, who knows how we are wired and all our weaknesses (103:13–14). This life may be as short and uncertain as the flowers of the field, here today and gone tomorrow, but God is eternal and the LORD's love for his people goes on 'from everlasting to everlasting' (103:17).

Is God really in charge of this world? Yes. 'He has established his throne in the heavens and his kingdom rules over all' (103:19). Earthly powers and empires come and go; history tells us that. But God is in control. He always has been and will remain so.

We praise God because of all that he has done and for the wonderful God he is. That is why the psalms call everyone and everything that God has made to join in praise of their maker and LORD (103:20, 21).

'Praise the LORD, my soul' (103:22).

Reflection

1. Read through Psalm 103 again. Try listing all the reasons you have to praise God and then turn that into worship.
2. Reflect on this command from Paul: 'Be joyful always; pray continually; give thanks in all circumstances, for this is God's will for you in Christ Jesus' (1 Thess 5:16).
3. Is this realistic in the face of all the problems we have to deal with? Why does Paul tell us to 'give thanks in all circumstances'?

34. THANKING GOD

Read Psalms 116 and 118

What shall I render unto the Lord for all his benefits towards me?
I will take the cup of salvation and call upon the name of the Lord
(116:12–13, KJV).

I was walking hurriedly to a meeting in the Sydney CBD recently when I stopped to look at a monument. It was not a particularly impressive sight, but what caught my attention was that, unusually for Australia I think, there was a Bible text clearly engraved. The monument, which stands on the corner of Bligh and Hunter streets, had been erected to commemorate the site of the first ever Christian sermon preached in Australia.

The preacher was the thirty-one-year-old evangelical chaplain Richard Johnson, the date was 3 February 1788 and the text was Psalm 116:12–13. No doubt he was reminding the people – sailors, traders, government officials and convicts – how much they had to be thankful for in their safe arrival with the First Fleet after a thirty-six-week voyage from England.

We are not told what the response was to the message, but it is a wonderfully simple text.

God has been good.

Question: What can I give him in return?

Answer: I will receive gladly his gracious offer of salvation, put my trust in him and direct my prayers of thanksgiving and prayers for daily strength to him.

Thankful for what?

The psalms are full of thankfulness to God. What are they so thankful for? To answer that, let's look at two psalms, Psalms 116 and 118, as examples.

The writer of Psalm 116 is thankful to God for answered prayer: 'He heard my cry for mercy'; 'When I was in great need, he saved me' (116:1, 6). This answer came in a time of great distress: 'The cords of death entangled me, the anguish of the grave came over me; I was overcome by trouble and sorrow. Then I called on the name of the Lord: "Lord save me."' (116:3–4).

He is also thankful that God is gracious and righteous and full of compassion (116:5). He then turns to remind himself again that the Lord has been good to him (116:7).

It is good to look back and remember how much we have to thank

God for. Some people keep journals as reminders. My mother-in-law used to write dates and notes of thanks to God in the column of her Bible to remind herself of times when God had answered prayers and helped her.

In Psalm 118, the psalmist is thankful for God's constant love: 'Give thanks to the LORD, for he is good; his love endures forever' (118:1). This was not just a creed he had learned from his parents or from religious teachers. He had proved its truth by inward conviction and outward evidence through hard experiences: 'When hard-pressed, I cried to the LORD; he brought me into a spacious place' (118:5).

The psalmist is thankful for God's presence and protection: 'The LORD is with me, I will not be afraid. What can mere mortals do to me? The LORD is with me; he is my helper' (118:6–7).

He is thankful for God's help and deliverance from his enemies: 'I was pushed back and about to fall, but the LORD helped me. The LORD is my strength and my defence; he has become my salvation' (118:13–14).

Thankful or complaining?

Even when we are not 'hard-pressed' and life is going well, grumbling, complaining and criticising others often comes very naturally to us. It shows us how wrapped up in ourselves we can be. When we get like that, it's a sign that we have forgotten God, how much he has given us and how much he has forgiven us.

By contrast, a thankful heart is evidence of God being at work in our lives. Thankfulness is not specifically listed in the New Testament as a gift of the Holy Spirit, or even as a fruit of the Holy Spirit, but it is most surely a mark of God's work in someone's life. Reading the psalms, and turning them into our own prayers, is a great way to make thankfulness to God part of our worship and part of life.

When times are good, let's thank God. When life is difficult and thanking God does not come so easily, we can still be thankful that God is good and his love will never end. So Psalm 118 ends: 'Give thanks to the LORD, for he is good; his love endures forever' (118:29).

Reflection

1. Athanasius wisely commented: 'The Psalms not only exhort us to be thankful, they also provide us with fitting words to say.'[36] Pause and thank God now for all his goodness to you, using the words of one or more of these psalms.

---

36 Athanasius, *Letter to Marcinellus*, p. 6.

2. 'What shall I return to the LORD for all his goodness to me' (116:12).
   What practical response does God want you to make?
3. What circumstances are challenging for you right now? What can you
   thank God for in the midst of them?

RELATIONSHIP

'A relationship with God is both corporate and individual. It holds together praise and prayer. It is both bodily expressed and inwardly felt.'[37]

Psalms expresses that relationship with God in all its dimensions. It uses a range of word pictures to help us understand the nature of the relationship of faith that God invites us into. He is our Saviour, Deliverer and Shield. He is also the Shepherd, the Light and the Rock.

The LORD is totally committed to our relationship with him; he is faithful to his promises and to his people.

---

37 Goldingay, *Psalms*, vol. 1, p. 58.

35. THE SHEPHERD

Read Psalm 23

The LORD is my Shepherd, I lack nothing (23:1).

Contentment

I have a book at home, picked up second hand at a book sale, by a seventeenth-century Puritan minister called Jeremiah Burroughs. Its title is *The Rare Jewel of Christian Contentment*. I think it would make an apt subtitle for Psalm 23.

Our ideas of contentment may involve relaxing with a cool drink and good book, or a long soak in a hot bath after a tiring day, but these types of contentment may quickly pass. One phone call from a troubled friend or a sick member of the family quickly breaks the spell.

This famous psalm, written by King David, paints a picture of a different kind of contentment: a deep, inner sense of 'shalom' in which one is right with God and the world and at peace with oneself.

This psalm has a very wide appeal and is often used at funerals, even of non-Christians. Why so? Because it is *comforting*, in the strongest sense of that word. It doesn't smooth over life's troubles or make light of them. It grapples with the experience of 'the darkest valley', yet finds comfort even there. It also appeals because it is *relational*. It assumes a relationship with God, who is the LORD who is the Shepherd and the friend. And, it ends on a very strong note of *confidence* that the relationship will go on into eternity.

Strength, dignity and confidence, the clothing of the godly woman in Proverbs 31, resonate throughout this beautiful psalm. No wonder God has used it to speak to so many people; no wonder so many readers discover for themselves the rare jewel of Christian contentment.

The Good Shepherd

Ancient Israel had many poor leaders who were supposed to lead and 'shepherd' the people but failed miserably. God, through his prophets, voiced his displeasure with them: 'Woe to the shepherds who are destroying and scattering the sheep of my pasture' (Jer 23:1; see also Ezek 34:2, 6).

By contrast, God himself is the Good Shepherd. He provides, protects and leads. Because of that knowledge, and secure in that relationship, the psalmist contentedly concludes, 'I lack nothing' (23:1).

I doubt that statement was true for David in material terms. He had a somewhat traumatic life. He lacked a settled home for many years; his life was frequently under threat; his family life was dysfunctional to say the least. But, in all that, he had a deep sense of security and satisfaction in his trust in God. That is why this psalm speaks to us even when we are sick, depressed or in trouble. When the chips are down, God will provide all that is ultimately worth having.

As the Good Shepherd, God provides good things for his flock. 'He makes me lie down in green pastures, he leads me beside quiet waters, he refreshes my soul' (23:2) is a beautiful picture of rural tranquillity. Even if we live in a crowded mega-city or in a parched desert, we can relate well to the experience described here. God provides for us. He gives us peace, rest and renewal. This is not a superficial rest brought about by relaxing on a tropical beach; it is peace in our souls, the peace that only God can give, the peace of acceptance, of sins forgiven and being right with him.

God, the Good Shepherd, also leads his flock to do right: 'He guides me along the right paths for his name's sake' (23:3). Our relationship with God has a strong moral dimension. He is always leading us to do that which is consistent with his name and character, even though we often wander off like foolish sheep (Isa 53:6).

But, what about the dark times; is the Good Shepherd still with us? What about in death itself when, 'all other guides turn back, and the traveller must go on alone.'[38] He has promised to still be there for us and with us, so we will not have to face death alone: 'Even though I walk through the darkest valley [the valley of the shadow of death] I will fear no evil for you are with me' (23:4).

The last time I saw my mother alive, I asked her if she was afraid to die. She was a Christian woman, and she looked me straight in the eye and said firmly, 'No!' I have treasured that memory ever since.

Confidence for the future

Notice how personal this psalm gets. The psalmist begins with statements *about* God: 'He makes me ... He leads me ... He restores me.' But then he begins to address it *to* God: 'You are with me, your rod and your staff, they comfort me' (23:4).

Notice also how the picture changes from the protection of a rural shepherd to participation in a great victory feast, at which the LORD

38 Kidner, *Psalms*, vol. 1, p. 111.

himself is the host (see also Lk 22:16): 'You prepare a table before me in the presence of my enemies; you anoint my head with oil, my cup overflows' (23:5).

That is the future, but what about now? The psalm ends on a great note of confidence: 'Surely your goodness and love will follow me all the days of my life, and I will live in the house of the LORD forever' (23:6).

'Surely': it is not a hopeful expression, as in, 'Surely the bus must come soon!' It is a statement of certainty based on the promise of God. God's goodwill and mercy, God's covenant love and faithfulness, will be my constant companion.

As we look to the LORD our Shepherd, so we will find that rare jewel, Christian contentment – and confidence that God is in charge of the future.

Reflection

1. What does this psalm about a country shepherd have to say to a twenty-first-century city dweller?
2. What are the things that cause you to worry and fear? How does this psalm address those fears?
3. Read Philippians 4:12. How was the Apostle Paul able to find contentment even while in prison?

36. THE LIGHT

Read Psalm 27

The LORD is my light and my salvation – whom shall I fear? (27:1).

Light and darkness

In this statement of faith, the writer reminds himself (and us) that because God is both a light and a strong deliverer, he has nothing to fear. But, as Goldingay points out, 'stating this somehow draws attention to the fact that evidently I *do* have reason for fear.'[39] The writer was going through a bad experience in which he felt cut off from God. He was afraid. The verses that follow describe attacks from 'evil men' (27:2–3), a 'day of trouble' (27:3) and the horror of being surrounded by enemies (27:6).

That is why this psalm, and others like it, speaks to us powerfully when we feel that evil is all round and that the world is lined up against us. It reminds us of the reality and power of God and all he has promised to be and do in our lives.

This psalm ends with one of the most wonderfully encouraging statements of faith to be found in all Scripture: 'I remain confident of this: I will see the goodness of the LORD in the land of the living' (27:14).

He is my light in the darkness. He is my salvation for this situation in which I am so fearful.

The light of God

God created light: 'And God said, "Let there be light," and there was light' (Gen 1:3).

And, God *is* light: it is the very essence of his being. As the New Testament tells us, 'God is light; in him there is no darkness at all' (1 Jn 1:5). Light represents truth and goodness. Darkness represents evil. Movies nearly always use light and darkness symbolically in this way. Scenes of cruelty and fear are usually shown in the darkness. Good things happen in the light.

When the psalmist says 'The LORD is my Light', he wants us to understand God as the source of all truth and love and power, one who shines his light to guide and teach and who dispels the darkness of ignorance, blindness and sin. The psalms also speak of the light of God's

---

39 Goldingay, *Psalms*, vol. 1, p. 392.

face and the light of his presence, illuminating our way and dispelling our darkness:

- 'For with you is the fountain of life; in your light we see light' (36:9).
- 'Light shines on the righteous and joy on the upright in heart' (97:11).
- 'Even in darkness, light dawns for the upright' (112:4).

Little children may be fearful of the dark and insist that the light is kept on while they go to sleep. The light takes away their fear. So when our trust is in God we can say with confidence, 'The LORD is my light and my salvation – whom shall I fear?' (27:1).

Guiding light

God was a literal 'guiding light' to Israel: 'He guided them with the cloud by day and with light from the fire all night' (78:14).

We are not promised visible supernatural signs such as those experienced by the children of Israel on their journey from Egypt to Canaan, but we are promised that God will guide us through his word and by his Holy Spirit: 'Your word is a lamp for my feet, a light on my path' (119:105) and, 'Send me your light and your faithful care, let them guide me' (43:3).

One of the most helpful books on God's guidance that I have ever read is Elisabeth Elliot's *God's Guidance: A Slow and Certain Light*. The title itself aptly pictures most of my experiences of divine guidance – not a blinding flash of certainty, but a gradual, growing and deepening conviction about the right path to follow as I have looked to the Lord for help.

The light of God's presence

We are also promised the light of the presence of God along the way: 'Blessed are those who have learned to acclaim you, who walk in the light of your presence, LORD' (89:15).

Jesus said that he is with us always, right up to the end. We are never alone.

When I was a student, we would sometimes go 'potholing' or 'caving'. We were well equipped with headlights much like small miner's lamps, but as we crawled through the underground limestone passages, they would sometimes fail. When the light goes out at fifty metres underground, the darkness is absolute. You cannot see your hand in front of your face. But the moment you switch on an emergency torch, the darkness is dispelled. That vivid picture has remained in my memory, and it is sparked whenever I read these words in John's Gospel: 'The light shines in the darkness, and the darkness has not overcome it' (Jn 1:5).

Sometimes the evil in this world can seem overwhelming, but the darkness can never defeat God and his good purposes for our life.

Reflection

1. In Psalm 27, why is David so thankful that God is his light?
2. Read Psalm 18:18. How does God turn our darkness into light?
3. The Apostle Paul uses the imagery of light and darkness to describe the change that God works in our lives in bringing us to faith in Christ: 'For God, who said, "Let light shine out of darkness," made his light shine in our hearts to give us the light of the knowledge of God's glory displayed in the face of Christ' (2 Cor 4:6).In what ways have you experienced the light of God shining into your life and guiding you?

37. THE ROCK

Read Psalms 18 and 62

The LORD is my rock, my fortress and my deliverer; my God is
my rock, in whom I take refuge, my shield and the horn of my
salvation, my stronghold (18:2).

Just after the big Indian Ocean tsunami of 2004, *The Australian Financial Review* carried a cartoon on its editorial page. It showed a desperate man in the ocean with a huge tidal wave about to break upon him. He was clearly in severe distress and he was clinging to a broken wooden cross on which was inscribed the word 'religion'.

The cartoonist was saying that in the face of disaster, people cling to religion. Even if religion is broken, it's all people have left. This view of religion is widely held in most Western countries, where the dominant values are material rather than spiritual. Religion is seen as a crutch, a support for weak-minded people who need it to get through life, and one to which even strong, self-sufficient people may turn in times of crisis.

But this is *not* how Christian faith is presented to us in the Bible. It is not a belief system created by humans to serve as a psychological prop to get us through life. It is a revelation of God as a person, who created the world and who calls us into a relationship with him, a relationship intended to last through time and eternity.

When natural disasters occur, whether the Indian Ocean tsunami, earthquakes in Japan or Nepal or volcanic eruptions in the Philippines, it makes even hardened atheists at least reflect on the fragility and uncertainty of existence, and of the meaning of life in the face of death.

As we turn to the psalms, we find people facing major crises. But there is no inadequate attempt to justify the ways of God, no carefully argued apologetic. No academic theological debate about the existence of God. Rather, there is the implicit assumption that God is there, he is in control and the buck stops with him. He is the one to turn to.

Our fortress

In such times of crisis in our lives, we find in the psalms an echo of our experiences. They point us to God as our fortress in time of attack. For example, Psalm 62 opens with this statement of faith: 'Truly my soul finds rest in God; my salvation comes from him. Truly he is my rock and my salvation; he is my fortress, I shall never be shaken' (62:1–2).

David, the author of Psalm 62, does not just trust in God alongside many other sources of help. Rather, his trust is truly, and only, in God. Remember, David was a soldier and a man of action. Though he was experienced in military tactics, and in using weapons during combat, he is not ashamed to make it clear that ultimately he relies one hundred percent on God.

This recognition is very important. We can build a whole series of supports in different compartments of our lives: our money, our work, our social lives, our reputations. But when crises come, we find there is no lasting security without God. It is not that God is there to rely on when we decide to turn to him ... He is the *only* rock, and all other support systems we rely on will eventually show themselves to be inadequate.

Our refuge

In the word pictures of Psalm 62, our God is likened to a rock, or refuge, to which we run for safety.

Picture with me a big rock outcrop near the top of a mountain: a position that can be readily defended with conventional weapons of war. Those being pursued by enemies can retreat back to the high ground, the rock from which they can see all their enemies and a vantage point from which they can repel all attacks. They are safe.

Salvation is being made safe. God is the rock to which we run to be made safe.

This picture recurs many times in Psalms:

- 'You are God my stronghold. Why have you rejected me?'
  (Psalm 43:2).
- 'You, God, are my fortress, my God on whom I can rely'
  (Psalm 59:9).
- 'Lead me to the rock that is higher than I' (Psalm 61:2).

If we dip back into the book of Proverbs, we find a similar statement of confident faith: 'The name of the LORD is a strong tower, the righteous runs into it and is safe' (4:18).

History tells us that all supposedly impregnable human fortresses can be breached, given the right combination of weapons, strategy and human resources. My wife's parents used to live near Corfe Castle in the south of England. The castle lies on the top of a hill at the junction of two valleys. It is reputed to have been a fortress even in Roman times, but the stone version was constructed in the eleventh century. At the time, it was virtually impregnable. Any would-be attackers approaching the castle could be clearly seen from a distance and easily picked off if they attempted to storm up the hill. Six hundred years later, the castle was virtually destroyed in the English civil War and now lies in partial ruins, no longer a fortress but a tourist attraction. By contrast, 'the fortress' that is our God is absolutely secure and indestructible. He lasts forever.

Sometimes our troubles drive us away from God. This psalm encourages us to let them drive us to him, to 'retreat' to God as our rock and our refuge.

Reflection

1. Augustus Toplady wrote the poem 'Rock of Ages' in 1776.[40]

   Rock of Ages, cleft for me,

   let me hide myself in thee;

   let the water and the blood,

   from the wounded side which flowed,

   be of sin the double cure,

   save from wrath and make me pure.

   What is the poet portraying in this first verse of the poem?

2. In what sense are we encouraged to hide ourselves in the Rock? See also Psalm 62:6–8.

---

40 This poem has been set to tune by a number of hymn-writers, most notably Thomas Hastings with the tune 'Toplady'.

38. THE FAITHFUL ONE

Read Psalm 89

I will sing of the LORD's great love forever; with my mouth I will
make your faithfulness known through all generations (89:1).

Love and faithfulness go together. As we have seen in Proverbs (see chapter
20), they form the basis of all strong human relationships. We are to bind
them around our necks and write them on the tablets of our hearts (Prov
3:3). That is, we are to keep them always 'front of mind' and embed them
deep into our souls.

They are the essentials for relationships because they are at the core of
God's character. Our best relationships are modelled on our relationship
with him.

Remembering God's promises

Psalm 89 is about the faithfulness of God. It is in four parts. The first part,
verses 1–18, comprises statements *about* God and statements made *to*
God, reminders of God's covenant with King David. In verses 19–37, God
himself is the speaker through the writer, but again the focus is on God's
covenant promises to David. The tone changes in verses 38–45 as the writer
looks at the shame being suffered by one of David's kingly successors. God
seems to have forgotten, or even renounced, his covenant. The psalm ends
at verses 46–51 with a prayer of questioning and pleading, all on the same
theme.

Throughout the psalm, the writer is looking back and remembering
God's promise to David, delivered through the prophet Nathan:

The LORD declares to you that the LORD himself will establish a
house for you: when your days are over and you rest with your
ancestors, I will raise up your offspring to succeed you, your own
flesh and blood, and I will establish his kingdom. He is the one who
will build a house for my Name and I will establish the throne of
his kingdom forever. I will be his father, and he shall be my son (2
Sam 7:11–14).

The people of Israel looked for the fulfilment of this promise in the kingly
line of David, but they were disappointed. Again and again the kings failed
to live up to Israel's expectations. Finally, when the young king Jehoachim
was deported to Babylon (2 Kgs 24:8), it seemed like the end of the line had

come and God had failed to keep his promise to David. This is the theme of Psalm 89:38–45. Then the writer turns away from this story of shame and failure, and turns to God to ask, 'How long, LORD? Will you hide yourself forever?' (89:46); 'Lord, where is your former great love, which in your faithfulness you swore to David? (89:49).

Waiting and trusting

In asking 'How long?' and getting no clear answer, this psalm finds an echo in every believer who has ever called on God to act and received no immediate response.[41]

With the benefit of historical perspective, and with the whole Bible in view, we can see how God's promise to David was fulfilled, not in the succession of the kings of Israel or of Judah, but in the coming of the Messiah – in the person of Jesus Christ. Humanly speaking, Jesus was a descendent of David, but he was also revealed as the Son of God.

It is always easier to see God's faithfulness when we look back. Looking forward, it is not so easy. As we face testing and painful times, when it seems as though God is not there, or that he is no longer being faithful to his promises to us, then we have to keep trusting as the psalmist did.

Actually, this psalmist does more than keep trusting. He also keeps praising, and he reminds both himself and his readers of God's promises as he does so. He begins with praise, a commitment to 'sing of the LORD's great love forever' (89:1). He also ends with praise, even though his questions are unanswered, because he *knows* God in the deepest sense of that word. He knows that God is loving and faithful, and the psalmist also knows that he must wait patiently to see visible evidence of that love working out in his experience and in answer to his prayers. So he ends, 'Praise be to the LORD forever! Amen and Amen' (89:52).

Faithfulness and love

How is the faithfulness of God to be understood? There are two sides to this particular coin. It is both faithfulness to a *promise* made and faithfulness to a *person* in a covenant relationship. In Christian marriage, these two come together because the promises made by each party seal the covenant. So each party promises, 'I will be faithful to you' (the person), and, 'I will by God's grace keep this promise that I have made' (the promise).

This is how we are to understand God's love and faithfulness. He is faithful to his promises; he is faithful to his people. Love and faithfulness

---

41 These 'How long?' questioning prayers are considered again in chapter 41

are inseparable in the character of God: 'I will declare that your love stands firm forever, that you have established your faithfulness in heaven itself' (89:2).

The test of any marriage or friendship is how it survives difficult times: arguments, financial pressures, health scares, the wear and tear of bringing up children, the stress of nursing sick or elderly relatives. Faithfulness and love in human relationships will always be tested. We may fail the tests and prove faithless and unloving, but God remains true to his promises to us.

One of the best-known statements about the faithfulness of God in all Scripture is found in the book of Lamentations, which paints a picture of otherwise unrelenting misery. These verses appear like a shaft of light in the darkness:

> Because of the LORD's great love we are not consumed, for his compassions never fail. They are new every morning; great is your faithfulness. I said to myself, 'The LORD is my portion; therefore I will wait for him.' The LORD is good to those whose hope is in him, to the one who seeks him; it is good to wait quietly for the salvation of the LORD. (Lam 3:22–26).

Reflection

1. How have you experienced the faithfulness of God in your life?
2. If you are struggling because of painful and stressful circumstances right now, read Psalm 89 and remind yourself continually of God's covenant promises.
3. Read Hebrews 6:12. How do faith and patience work together?

PRAYER

'Most of Scripture speaks *to* us, while the psalms speak *for* us.'[42]

John Goldingay opens his book, *Songs from a Strange Land*, with this perceptive comment. His acknowledged inspiration for this insight is the fourth-century Christian leader Athanasius, who expressed the same idea more fully in these words:

> The reader takes all its words upon his lips as though they were his own and each one sings the Psalms as though they had been written for his special benefit, and takes them and recites them, not as though someone else were speaking or another person's feeling being described, but as himself speaking of himself, offering the words to God as his own heart's utterance, just as though he himself had made them up.[43]

Anyone who has read Psalms and found there a prayer that seems to exactly fit their emotional state, or mirror their experience of pain, fear or perplexity, knows exactly what Athanasius meant.

One writer has suggested that all of the psalms can be divided into two categories, praise and lament, to correspond to the two human emotions of joy and suffering.[44] That may be an oversimplification, but there are certainly many prayers in Psalms that believers down the years have made their own, allowing the psalms to speak *for* them, as well as *to* them. Here we look at some of those prayers: prayers that express a longing for God, hope for a new start or the desire to be whole; prayers that question God in times of trouble or cry to him for help and for justice; and prayers in which the writer seems to be talking to himself, rather than to God.

---

42 Goldingay, *Songs from a Strange Land*, p. 17.
43 Athanasius, *Letter to Marcinellus.*
44 Westermann, *The Living Psalms*, p. 10.

39. LONGING FOR GOD

Read Psalms 42 and 63

As the deer pants for streams of water, so my soul pants for you, my God. My soul thirsts for God, for the living God. Where can I go and meet with God? (42:1–2).

Water and life

Drought is a terrible thing. In Australia, and in many countries in Africa, it threatens the lives of people and animals, destroys wealth, and puts great strain on relationships and people's well-being.

The sight of dried-up dams and waterholes, with dead animals lying in the heat of the sun on hard-baked, cracked earth, is all too common to farmers and graziers in times of drought.

During a drought, we look to the heavens in hope of rain. Day after day, we long for water. The earth itself seems to cry out for water. Without water, there is no life. Without water to drink, we die.

Without the knowledge of God and the Spirit of God, we are spiritually dead. The psalmists frequently use this powerful analogy of a thirst for water to express longing for God: 'I thirst for you like a parched land' (143:6).

Thirsty for God

The writer of Psalm 42 must have seen the effects of drought in nature, and he could identify that experience with the state of his own spiritual life. He felt dried up spiritually and thirsty for an experience of God that would satisfy his deep longing: 'My soul thirsts for God, for the living God. Where can I go and meet with God?' (42:1–2).

The reason for his thirst is the sustained mockery of non-believers, who are asking all day long, 'Where is your God?' (42:3, 10). Having publicly affirmed his faith, the psalmist is vulnerable to such attacks at times when God's blessing is not obvious. Further, having known God, he knows that nothing else and no-one else can quench his thirst for spiritual reality.

Whatever success we have in life – in work, in art or leisure, even in marriage and family – it cannot satisfy the desire God has planted in our souls to know our Creator.

I have experienced several 'dry times' in my life, times when God has seemed far away and when I have had little inclination to pray, read the Bible or worship. Those dry times have led me to long for what I once had, and then, thank God, on to recovery and the renewal of my faith.

During those down times, I could identify with this psalmist. He looks back longingly to great times of worship and celebration with God's people, but now feels downcast, disturbed and depressed (42:4–5). And yet, he still turns to God in prayer, by day and night (42:8); he continues to affirm his trust in God and encourages himself to keep trusting and hoping, knowing that God will satisfy his thirst.

'I will yet praise him, my Saviour and my God' (42:11).

Satisfaction

Psalm 63 expresses a similar longing for spiritual reality, to find and know God.

'You God, you are my God, earnestly I seek you; I thirst for you, my whole body longs for you, in a dry and parched land where there is no water' (63:1).

This longing for God is not that of a stranger. It is like the longing of a friend or a lover – a longing to know our Creator who has first loved us. In Augustine's famous words, 'You stir man to take pleasure in praising you, because you have made us for yourself and our heart is restless until it rests in you.'[45]

The world can never satisfy that restless longing, nor can any man-made religion. This is a thirst to know God. It is a longing with great singleness of purpose.

Have you ever been seriously thirsty? Perhaps while lying in hospital awaiting an operation with the label 'nil by mouth' on the foot of your bed? Or bushwalking in the heat when you forgot to pack enough water? When we are *really* thirsty, only water will do – not coffee, spirits, wine or juice. When we long for God, only knowing his presence in our lives will satisfy us. No other religious substitutes will do. In the midst of this experience of spiritual dryness, when the writer is longing for a new touch from God, he wisely lets his thoughts and prayers take him in three directions. Let's learn from him.

First, he *looks back* to experiences of God's presence and power, now gone but not forgotten: 'I have seen you in the sanctuary and beheld your power and your glory' (63:2).

---

45 Augustine, *Confessions*, p. 3.

Then, he reaffirms his belief in the unfailing and unchanging love of God as a *present reality*: 'your love is better than life' (63:3).

Finally, because of that love, he commits himself to continuing to praise God and honour him *in the future*: 'my lips will glorify you. I will praise you as long as I live' (63:3–4).

Looking back with thankfulness, looking forward with hope and living in the present in faith and commitment – what a great way to live!

The invitation of Jesus

Jesus, the Son of God, used the same analogy of the necessity of water to produce and sustain life. He claimed life-giving power in these words of promise and invitation:

Everyone who drinks this water will be thirsty again, but whoever drinks the water I give them will never thirst, Indeed, the water I give them will become in them a spring of water welling up to eternal life (Jn 4:13–14);

> Let anyone who is thirsty come to me and drink. Whoever believes in me, as the Scripture has said, rivers of living water will flow from within them (Jn 7:37).

No-one will ever make a greater promise to us than this. Let us hold on to it and thank God for it. No-one will ever give us a better invitation. Let us gratefully accept.

Reflection

1. The prayer in Psalm 63 begins with a longing to commune with God and know him better. Read this psalm and make it your prayer today.
2. Read Isaiah 35. What pictures does it paint of the life-giving effects of water?
3. How does Paul express his spiritual longing in Philippians 4:7–10?

40. A NEW START

Read Psalm 51

Create in me a pure heart, O God, and renew a steadfast spirit
within me (51:10).

The problem

When we mess up, whether in an exam paper, work task or relationship,
we long for a new start. We long to begin again, to start over so that we can
get it right.

David, the author of Psalm 51, desperately wanted a new start.

He had committed the double sin of adultery with the wife of one of his
loyal soldiers, and then, in a futile attempt at cover-up, plotted the death of
her husband! David had been confronted with his crimes by the prophet
Nathan and now was deeply troubled by his wrongdoing. He felt loaded
down with guilt and a sense of failure as he struggled to come to terms
with the fatal flaw in his make-up that had caused him to do such evil. He
had done something he knew was wrong, but his sinful nature led him to
do it anyway.

That knowledge and that guilt led David to cry to God for mercy – to
blot out his transgressions (51:1) and wash him clean from the inner dirt
in his life, his 'iniquity' (51:2).

David also recognised another dimension to his problem, the most
important dimension of all: 'Against you, you only, have I sinned' (51:4). He
realised that he had offended God. He had rebelled against the authority of
God and rejected God's love.

In this psalm, as David reflects on the mess in his life, his lack of inner
peace and his constant failure to change and improve, he acknowledges the
root cause of his problem: 'Surely I was sinful at birth, sinful from the time
my mother conceived me' (51:5).

Most of us are painfully aware of things we have said and done that
we wish we hadn't. Most of us will also admit the weaknesses in our
characters that lead us to do and say the wrong thing. Yet we may stop
short of confessing our sin to God or admitting our accountability to him.
It is rather like a person with a malignant tumour denying that there is
anything seriously wrong.

Honesty: the way forward

What is the way forward? Well-meaning advice to lighten up and focus on the positives won't cut it. Honesty is the best policy! David realised that God wants us to be honest about our lives.

He asks God to 'blot out' (51:1) his transgressions, as though cleaning an ink stain from a garment; to 'wash away' (51:2) his iniquity, which is spoiling and defiling him; and to 'cleanse' (51:2) him from sin.

In this, David is asking God, not merely to deal with the surface dirt – the effects of sin – but also to deal with his deeper problems. He knows that if he continues to do what he has always done, he will get the same result he has always got. Something has to change radically.

He returns later to this deep longing for change: 'Cleanse me with hyssop and I shall be clean; wash me and I will be whiter than snow' (51:7). He wants to be a new person, with even the memory of past failures forgotten and totally forgiven. He wants to experience the re-creative power of God in his life: 'Let me hear joy and gladness; let the bones you have crushed rejoice' (51:8).

He wants an inner purity and an inner strength that he knows can't be found within himself. He wants also the blessing of the conscious, constant presence of God: 'Do not cast me from your presence or take your Holy Spirit from me' (51:11).

David had known the experience of God's blessing on his life; now, he had lost it. So he prays: 'Restore to me the joy of your salvation and grant me a willing spirit to sustain me' (51:12).

He also prays that God will again use him in doing something useful with his life: 'Then I will teach transgressors your ways so that sinners will be brought back to you' (51:13).

Does this psalm resonate with you? You may never have failed as spectacularly as David or committed the gross sins of murder and adultery. You may be a respected Christian or even a leader in your Christian community. Others may look to you and think you have your life together, but you know that it is not true. You have no peace with God and you don't feel good. You seem to lapse back into the well-worn rut of past failings, and you are weighed down with unresolved issues and unconfessed sin.

Maybe it's time to start being honest with God and with yourself; to confess your sin and ask God for a clean heart and a new start.

Too good to be true?

David asks for a radical change to his character: 'Create in me a pure heart, O God, and renew a steadfast spirit within me' (51:10).

Is this possible? We usually find it difficult to erase past failures from the memory banks of our consciences.

In the financial world, if someone offers you a deal or an investment opportunity that sounds too good to be true, then it usually is. People may lose their life savings to 'scammers' who paint an unrealistic picture of the likely returns.

But the gospel promises a new start. It all sounds 'too good to be true', but it *is* true. When God offers us a new start with the past forgiven and forgotten, and with his Spirit renewing us and strengthening us each day, then let's accept it. It is the best gift we will ever receive.

Reflection

1. What would you say to someone who thinks that all talk of sin is negative and unhelpful?
2. What is David's response to God's forgiveness? (51:15).
3. If you feel in need of a new start right now, then read Psalm 51 and make it your own prayer.

41. QUESTIONING GOD

Read Psalms 10, 22 and 74

Why, LORD, do you stand far off? Why do you hide yourself in
times of trouble? (10:1).
Why does the wicked man revile God? Why does he say to
himself, 'He won't call me to account'? (10:13).

The psalms are full of questions. They pose questions to God in prayers,
asking *why* he has allowed the particular difficulty or pain or injustice they
are experiencing, or *how long* they must wait before God decides to answer
their prayers. Sometimes the psalmists address their questions to no-one
in particular, voicing their queries aloud without seeming to expect an
answer.

The 'why' questions

Why? We might whisper that question through our tears as we wonder
why God allowed that car crash to happen. We might voice it aloud in
conversation with friends, without necessarily wanting to hear their
answers. We might shout it aloud to God, angered by the suffering of
innocent children at the hands of terrorists. The writers of Psalms had no
problem in asking God, 'Why?'

'Why have you forsaken me?' (22:10).

'Why do you hold back your hand, your right hand?' (74:11).

'O God, why have you rejected us forever? Why does your anger
smoulder against the sheep of your pasture?' (74:10).

When we look at the psalms in which each of these questions appear, we
find that none of them are answered in the way the writer wants. Although
we naturally like to interrogate God, calling him to account for his actions
(or inaction), God does not often respond when we want him to or in ways
we would like him to.

In Psalm 10, the writer is grappling with the familiar question: why do
evil people who reject God seem to do so well? The writer is looking for all
wrongs to be righted in *this* life. God, it seems, has an eternal perspective
on justice.

Psalm 22 expresses feelings of personal rejection. The fact that Jesus
spoke its opening words during the agony of the cross shows us something

of the depth of his spiritual anguish as well as his horrendous physical suffering: 'I am poured out like water, and all my bones are out of joint. My heart has turned to wax; it has melted within me' (22:14).

Psalm 74 appears to have been written after the Babylonian destruction of Jerusalem in 587 BC, which left the whole nation devastated and asking why God had rejected them and allowed their enemies to humiliate them: 'We are given no signs from God; no prophets are left, and none of us knows how long this will be' (74:9). God's people have been defeated, their holy place has been destroyed and their God is being laughed at (74:10). Why has God seemingly left his people to face this onslaught of evil alone?

But it's not all 'gloom and doom'. Both psalms look back to better times, when God delivered his people (22:4) and redeemed them and made them his own (74:2). Both affirm the total sovereignty of God over all his world (22:27 and 74:12).

The 'how long' questions

'How long, LORD? Will you forget me forever?' (13:1).

'How long will the enemy mock you, God?' (74:10).

'How long, LORD? Will you hide yourself forever? (89:46).

How long do I have to wait before God answers my prayer for a job, a marriage partner, a child, healing? How long do I have to put up with this difficult situation? Peter Adam has commented: 'The prayer "how long" is a wonderful prayer. It is the prayer of someone who has turned to God yet again for help.'[46]

As with the 'why' questions, these 'how long' questions are being asked both by the individual (Psalm 13) and by the community (74:10). And again, there is no direct answer. But in both prayers we find the writers finding some peace in remembering God (74:1) and how good he has been in the past (74:13–16). Psalm 13 goes one step further. It turns from questions to statements and commitments of faith: 'But I trust in your unfailing love; my heart rejoices in your salvation. I will sing the LORD's praise, for he has been good to me' (13:6).

The rhetorical questions

Psalm 77 is yet another cry of a man in distress, one whose soul 'refused to be comforted' (77:2), one who is too troubled to speak (77:44) and feels God has rejected him. 'Will the Lord reject forever? Will he never show

---

46 From a talk on Habakkuk given by Peter Adam at the Spring Young Minister's Conference, 2015: www.proctrust.org.uk.

his favour again? Has his unfailing love vanished forever? Has his promise failed for all time? Has God forgotten to be merciful? Has he in anger withheld His compassion?' (77:7–9).

More questions – but rhetorical questions, for which the psalmist, deep in the pit, seems neither to expect nor want answers. Yet, as the questioner starts to think about God, he *does* find answers to his questions: in remembering who God is and what he has done, what he has promised, and therefore what he will do. The psalmist may have lost his grip on these realities, but he finds it again: 'I will meditate on all your works and consider your mighty deeds' (77:12).

Moving closer to God

God is surely telling us something here. When we are wrestling with doubt and depression, questioning ourselves and God, when the last thing we actually want is a response from well-meaning friends in the form of platitudinous statements which fail to touch us or relieve our pain, there is still a way out of the pit of despair. Like the psalmists, we are wise to look back to God's work in the past, both in our own lives and in history, and to look up to God himself and remember he is still there. He is still the same. He is big enough to handle all our questions.

Pain, pressure or unanswered prayer may drive us away from God. But the psalms show us how they can drive us *to* God instead. They help us move beyond a merely superficial faith into a deeper relationship of trust.

Reflection

1. When you are struggling to see why God has brought dark times to your life, then get alone into a quiet place and read Psalm 77 out aloud. Make this psalm your own.
2. Read Psalm 2, with its question in verse 1. How does the rest of the psalm answer that question?

42. SEARCHING FOR WHOLENESS

Read Psalm 86

Give me an undivided heart, that I may fear your name (86:11).

The heart of the problem

Little children have a very direct way of letting their parents know their needs: 'I'm hungry!', 'I'm tired!', 'Can you carry me?'

Sometimes our prayers to God have a similar directness and urgency. So it is with Psalm 86: 'Hear me, LORD, and answer me, for I am poor and needy' (86:1). David, who wrote this prayer, has no difficulty telling God what he wants him to do!

In the first four verses of this psalm, there are five specific requests: 'hear me', 'guard my life', 'save your servant', 'have mercy on me', and 'bring joy'. More focused requests come later: 'teach me your way', 'turn to me', 'show your strength', and 'give me a sign of your goodness' (86:11–17). He prays for a visible, tangible sign that God is with him.

But one specific request in the middle of this psalm gets to the heart of the problem:

'Teach me your way, LORD, that I may rely on your faithfulness; give me an undivided heart, that I may fear your name' (86:11).

A divided heart

David has come to God with a list of personal needs. But after praying for a while and reflecting on the character of God, he sees that he has one big problem that towers above the others: the problem of his own heart, his inner self. His heart is 'divided'; it is pulled in different directions. His loyalties are split. He longs to have a sense of wholeness, of his whole being moving in one direction.[47]

We usually admire people who are very focused in their pursuit of their personal goals: sportspeople who want to win, business people who want to make lots of money, actors and singers wanting success and fame. This prayer expresses a longing for the same sort of single-minded devotion, but in pursuit of a deeper relationship with God.

When the Spirit of God works in our lives to show us the shallowness, pointlessness and emptiness of life without God, then we start to be pulled

---

47   For further reading, see my book *Undivided: Closing the Faith–Life Gap*.

in two directions: to love God or to follow human instinct, which is, as my elder sister used to remind me, 'Me first, me second and – if there is any left over – me third!'

We experience this internal 'tug of war' in our thinking: is what the Bible says true, or should we believe the latest sensational novelist or pundit on TV? We sense it in our emotions and desires: one minute we long to be a good person, and the next we can cut down our dearest loved ones with angry words. We feel it in our decision-making: we can resolve on Sundays at worship that we want to live God's way, but at work on Monday morning we fall back to the 'everyone for themselves' approach to life in the jungle.

We also experience this dividedness in our actions. In the language of sports coaches and business leaders, 'we fail to execute'. Even after we have decided in our minds that we want to do the right thing, even after our emotions are stirred by the love of God and our wills are firmly resolved, it can all quickly go wrong. We can resolve to contact that lonely person, but life gets too busy and we forget. Or, we decide to give our time to a volunteer care group but low self- esteem and worry that what we do won't be good enough stops us. We had the 'game plan', the desire and the intent, but we failed to put it into practice.

The problem is that we have a divided heart. We are people pulled in different directions in our thinking, emotions, decisions and actions. We need wholeness. But how?

Higher ground

In Psalm 86, David gets up from prayer, as we ourselves often do, with no definite answer. But he does get up strengthened in his faith. He has his eyes back on God. He has remembered that God is in control, and he is ready to face life again, secure in that knowledge.

The psalm begins in the valley of need, but 'the prayer resolutely heads towards clearer skies and firmer ground'.[48] The way to that firmer ground is for us, like David, to bring our life, our *whole* life, under the control of God; to ask God to work in our lives by His Spirit to unite what is divided within us. He had prayed for an undivided heart but he moved onwards and upwards with great confidence and joy to affirm: 'I will praise you, Lord my God, with *all my heart*; I will glorify your name forever. For great is your love towards me' (86:11–12, italics mine).

---

48 Kidner, *Psalms*, vol. 2, p. 311.

Reflection

1. Read Psalm 86 again, noting all the reminders about the goodness of God. How does reminding ourselves of God's goodness help with the problem of a divided heart?
2. How does the New Testament express the problem of a divided heart and how can we find wholeness? See Romans 7:14–25; Galatians 5:16–25.
3. The following verse, from a hymn by Thomas Ken, seems to capture the intent of Psalm 86. You may like to make this your prayer:

   > Direct, control, suggest this day,
   > all I desire or do or say
   > that all my powers, with all their might
   > for your sole glory may unite.[49]

---

49 Thomas Ken, *Awake, My Soul, and with the Sun* 1674.

43. CRYING OUT FOR HELP

Read Psalms 69, 88 and 107

Save me, O God, for the waters have come up to my neck. I sink in
the miry depths, where there is no foothold (69:1–2).

We often politely *ask* the LORD for help in our prayers. What would it take
for you to *cry out* to God to save you?

When we lived in Papua New Guinea, we were robbed three times. It
was a common experience. A doctor friend of ours described his experience
of being attacked by burglars at his home in the highlands town of Goroka.
The intruders tied up his wife, and he found himself lying on the floor with
his hands pinned behind his back as two of the attackers threatened him
with large knives.

Our friend told us how he learned in that experience what it meant to cry
out aloud to God for help. 'Lord, *save me!*' he shouted, quite unashamedly.
Whether that surprised his attackers or not, he was happy to report that
God answered that cry. The burglars ransacked the house for valuables, but
they left him and his wife unharmed.

Desperation

The author of Psalm 69 had been through a desperate, life-threatening
experience. This is the cry of someone absolutely at the end of their tether.
They had tried prayer, and it seems to have failed; God appeared not to be
listening and was nowhere to be found.

'I am worn out calling for help; my throat is parched. My eyes fail
looking for my God' (69:3).

The writer is surrounded by enemies. Inside, he is a mass of guilt and
shame. His family has rejected him (69:8) and he is an object of scorn,
abuse and bad jokes by the local drunks (69:12).

But, paradoxically, the writer has not given up on prayer. Neither has
he given up trusting in the goodness and faithfulness of God, even though
he has no evidence of it in his present experience. There is a turning point:
'But I pray to you, LORD, in the time of your favour; in your great love, O
God, answer me with your sure salvation' (69:13). He prays for God to
answer (69:13, 16) and rescue him: 'Rescue me from the mire'; 'Come near
and rescue me' (69:14, 18).

Then, as in so many other psalms, the focus on God in prayer moves to praise and confidence that God will keep his covenant promises and not forsake us in time of need (69:30–36).

Beyond blue

Beyond Blue is an Australian initiative to reduce the impact of anxiety, depression and suicide in the community.[50] The writer of Psalm 88 is certainly 'beyond blue'. He is way past just feeling depressed: 'I am overwhelmed with troubles and my life draws near to death' (88:3); 'I am like one without strength (88:4); 'You have put me in the lowest pit, in the darkest depths' (88:6).

He is feeling totally alone: 'You have taken from me my closest friends and have made me repulsive to them' (88:8).

He feels that God is not listening to his cries for help and has rejected him, 'Why, LORD, do you reject me and hide your face from me?' (88:14). He concludes: 'darkness is my closest friend' (88:18).

There is no triumphalist answer or simplistic fix to the deep depression in this psalm. Sometimes life feels like that. We are beyond well-meaning advice, happy worship songs or platitudes. But the truth remains: God does not leave us in our deepest need.

Author Corrie Ten Boom discovered this in the dark horror of a Nazi concentration camp. Her beloved sister Betsy, who was close to death, was confident that Corrie would survive. She urged Corrie to take the message of the love of God to people after the war ended: 'We must tell people what we have learned here. We must tell them that there is no pit so deep that He is not deeper still.' She added, 'They will listen to us, Corrie, because we have been here.'[51]

Unfailing love

What happens when God does answer our desperate cry for help and bring us relief? Do we forget it and move on? Do we tell people it was just good luck, coincidence or 'the way things turned out'? Psalm 107 is a reminder to stop and thank God when he answers prayer.

The writer looks back on history and looks around his world to people crying out to God for help in desperate situations. There are refugees with no home (107:4–9), prisoners (107:10–16), travellers and working people (107:23–32).

---

50 www.beyondblue.org.au.
51 Corrie Ten Boom, *The Hiding Place*, p. 240.

In each case the psalm encourages us, like a chorus repeated through a song: 'Then they cried out to the LORD in their trouble, and he delivered them from their distress (107:6, 13, 19, 28). 'Let them give thanks to the LORD for his unfailing love and his wonderful deeds for mankind' (107:8, 15, 21, 31).

Reading Psalm 107 again as I wrote this reflection, I was reminded about the urgent prayer offered by our family for a baby in the womb who had seemingly stopped growing at six months. This had been confirmed by repeated examinations. Two weeks later, the baby had grown a massive seven hundred grams. Was that coincidence, a technical error in earlier scans or 'just the way things turned out'? As for our family, we believed it was the gracious work of God responding to our cry for help, and we joined this psalmist in giving thanks to the LORD for his unfailing love.

When we are going through really dark times, when we feel desperate, let's not be afraid or ashamed to cry out to God.

Reflection

1. What times have there been in your life when you have cried out to God for help?
2. If you are struggling right now such that you can hardly find words to pray, try reading Psalm 69.
3. Psalm 107 ends with a statement: 'Let the one who is wise heed these things and ponder the loving deeds of the LORD' (107:43). Take a few moments to look back over the times God has obviously answered your prayers, and give thanks to him for his unfailing love.

44. TALKING TO OURSELVES

Read Psalms 43 and 62

Why, my soul, are you downcast? (43:5).

Talking to ourselves is not always the first sign of madness! When we see close-ups on our TV screens of athletes at major sporting events, we often see them talking to themselves. Sometimes an audible question after a mistake: 'what *are* you doing?'; sometimes a muttered reminder of their coach's instruction: 'Keep your head still, watch the ball ... watch the ball!'; sometimes a shout or a scream heard by the whole crowd: 'Come *on*! Fire up!'

In Psalms, talking to ourselves, whether in the form of a question, a quiet self-encouragement or a loud shout, is a sign of spiritual health – a way of lifting ourselves out of the pit of self-pity and depression.

A question

Psalms 42 and 43, which seem to be a pair, both end with the writer asking himself a question and then encouraging himself with the answer: 'Why, my soul, are you downcast? Why so disturbed within me? Put your hope in God, for I will yet praise him, my Saviour and my God' (43:5).

Well, maybe this is not so much an answer as a reminder that God still cares and an encouragement to press on and keep trusting.

Dr Martyn Lloyd-Jones, the well-known Welsh preacher and former physician, frequently advocated the practice of talking to oneself in the style of Psalms.

> The main art in this matter of spiritual living is to know how to handle yourself. You have to take yourself in hand, you have to address yourself, preach to yourself, question yourself. You must say to your soul: '*Why* art thou cast down' – what business have you to be disquieted? You must turn on yourself upbraid yourself, condemn yourself, exhort yourself, and say to yourself: 'Hope thou in God' – instead of muttering in this depressed, unhappy way. And then you must go on to remind yourself of God, Who God is, and what God is and what God has done, and what God has pledged Himself to do. Then having done that, end on this great note: defy yourself, and defy other people, and defy the devil and the whole world and say with this man: 'I shall yet praise Him for the help of

His countenance', He, 'who is also the health of my countenance and my God'.[52]

When we are down, we tend to *listen* to ourselves – to our moans and grumbling and criticisms – and wrap ourselves around with self-pity and discouraging thoughts. The way out is to *talk* to ourselves instead!

A quiet encouragement

We find a slightly different example of a writer talking to himself in Psalm 62.

'Yes, my soul, find rest in God; my hope comes from him. Truly, he is my rock and my salvation; he is my fortress, I will not be shaken. My salvation and my honour depend on God; he is my mighty rock, my refuge' (62:5–7).

Here is a psalm that contains a mix of prayers, requests, reminders and statements of faith. At the beginning, the psalmist states his conviction: 'Truly my soul finds rest in God' (62:1), but then, as he considers all the forces raging against him and the people taking personal aim at him with malicious intent, perhaps his faith starts to waver (62:3–4). He feels the need for a 'note to self', a reminder that God is his rest: 'Yes, my soul, find rest in God; my hope comes from him' (62:5).

Shout out loud

Another style of 'talking to oneself' comes not in the form of a question or a quiet encouragement, but in more of a 'shout out loud' challenge: 'Praise the LORD, my soul; all my inmost being, praise his holy name. Praise the LORD, my soul, and forget not all his benefits' (103:1–2).

This is an internal 'gee-up', a spurring on, a rallying cry, to remember all that God has done in the world and in our own lives. It begins and ends with the writer reminding himself to 'praise' (literally 'bless') the LORD. Goldingay comments, 'The Psalm's framework is an exhortation to worship addressed to the self ... and eventually to the supernatural and natural worlds.'[53]

This is a great technique to use when we don't feel like praising God, when we have become so bogged down in our problems and priorities that we have forgotten the LORD and his goodness. If we have taken our eyes off him, then this is a sure antidote to that problem.

---

52 Lloyd-Jones, *Spiritual Depression*, p. 21.
53 Goldingay, *Psalms*, vol. 3, p. 165.

As we pray through situations facing us, and as we reflect on the promises of God in the Bible, let's make it part of our practice to talk to ourselves, questioning ourselves and encouraging ourselves, so that we may find our strength in the LORD. As we do that, we will find that we are much better equipped to help others along the way.

Reflection

1. In what sort of situations and in what ways do you talk to yourself?
2. After reading these psalms, identify some positive ways of talking to yourself that could help you in your walk of faith.

45. DEMANDING JUSTICE

Read Psalms 35 and 109

May all who gloat over my distress be put to shame and confusion
(35:26).

The desire for revenge it deeply embedded in human nature. In its purest form, it is a cry for justice: for the guilty to be punished and wrongs to be righted. In its worst form, it is vindictive hatred, boiling over into cruel intent. The desire for revenge has kept many personal and family feuds going that should have been settled long ago. It is what keeps wars going between Israel and the Palestinians, Shiite and Sunni Muslims, and Protestants and Catholics in Northern Ireland. In Papua New Guinea, where I worked for five years, the concept and practice of 'payback' is a cultural norm in many of the tribal groups, a so-called matter of honour, but it is one that continues to fan the flames of many intertribal and interpersonal disputes.

Many psalms contain cries for God to act, which, to our ears, sound shocking, offensive and un-Christian. Yet we find that there are some twenty-five psalms that scholars call 'imprecatory': that is, they contain prayers to God to take vengeance on the psalmists' enemies. How are we to interpret them? Are these prayers ones that we should pray, in the same way we may make other prayers in the psalms our own?

Context first!

Before we jump to conclusions, let's remember to look at the context of these psalms.

Firstly, David, like other writers of the psalms, experienced a lot of personal injustice, particularly from Saul and his followers who were simply jealous of David. He knew what it was to be falsely accused, suffer malicious personal attacks and be pursued by bands of men actively committed to killing him. As one brought up on the law of God, many of David's prayers are along the lines of 'do to them as they wanted to do to me' (Deut 19:19). With David, these imprecatory psalmists seek retributive action from God, asking that their enemies experience similar to what they themselves had suffered, but not beyond.

Secondly, these are prayers asking *God* to act. They do not describe actions actually taken, or intended to be taken, by the writer. We need to contrast these prayers with David's noble actions. One two occasions when he was hiding from Saul, it seemed that God had given him a unique opportunity to take his revenge and kill Saul. Indeed, David's men urged him to take advantage of the opportunity which it seemed God had provided. David declined, saying 'The LORD forbid that I should do such a thing to my master, the LORD's anointed' (1 Sam 24:6). David clearly knew that revenge was God's prerogative, not his.[54]

Thirdly, and perhaps mostly importantly, these psalms were written before the fuller revelation of God given to us in Jesus Christ concerning our response to those who wrong us, and in the fuller revelation of the truth that God's justice is worked out, not just in this age, but in eternity.

Is it right to pray these prayers?

We recognise that many of the psalm prayers are not nice, polite Christian prayers. As we have seen, they are cries from the depths of the heart, cries for help in desperate situations, cries of anguish: 'How long must I endure this?' Let us not be surprised, therefore, that there are psalms that voice a human longing to pay back for hurts and wrongs. After all, we are invited to 'pour out [our] hearts to him' (62:8), to tell God *honestly* what we are thinking and how we are feeling.

At one level, perhaps these prayers are there to help us 'get it all out there': to voice the desire for revenge that can boil up out of our hearts, aiding us in venting our spleen and letting off steam. Perhaps God, having listened to this, then says to us: 'I will sort out the injustice; I will sort out those who have unjustly harmed you. But you … you pray for them.'

The problem is that because we are sinful, our desire for justice inevitably gets mixed up and polluted by our personal desire for revenge. I, for one, am not sure I can pray for this sort of justice without getting angry and falling into sin.

Whether or not we use these prayers to tell God our true feelings, we need to heed the command of Jesus to 'Love your enemies and pray for those who persecute you' (Mt 5:44), a command he himself obeyed when he prayed for those who were nailing him to a cross: 'Father forgive them, they do not know what they are doing' (Lk 23:34).

Perhaps the final word on this matter of demanding justice is in Paul's letter to the Romans:

> Do not repay anyone evil for evil … Do not take revenge, my dear
> friends, but leave room for God's wrath, for it is written: 'It is mine

---

54 On some occasions though, David *did* take revenge. He had a violent streak and was certainly not a perfect example in this respect.

to avenge; I will repay,' says the Lord ... Do not be overcome by evil,
but overcome evil with good (Rom 12:17–21).

Reflection

1. Read Hebrews 12:14–15: what 'bitter roots', what hurts and resentments,
   are growing in your life? How can you deal with them?
2. Start praying for the good of those who have hurt you. Of course, it is
   hard – but it is what Jesus did and what he calls us to do.

46. ANSWERED PRAYER

Read Psalm 34

I sought the LORD, and he answered me; he delivered me from all
my fears (34:4).

In my early thirties, during a two-year break from my work in a global
infrastructure business, I had the privilege of studying Old Testament (and
some Hebrew!) under Alec Motyer, a renowned Old Testament scholar
and preacher based in the United Kingdom. He called this psalm 'an A to
Z for a time of trouble', because it is an alphabet acrostic poem – each of the
twenty-two verses begins with one of the twenty-two letters of the Hebrew
alphabet. It would have been a great aid for those wanting to memorise the
psalm in the original language. We are told in the heading to this psalm
that David wrote it after he had escaped from the court of the Philistines.
He was being threatened by his enemies and feigned madness to escape (1
Sam 21:10–15). Looking back on this low point in his life, when his faith
nearly failed him, he concluded that God had heard his cry for help and
delivered him from this life-threatening situation. So he wrote this psalm
about the goodness of the LORD who answers prayer.

God is listening

Alec would also point out the significance of the Hebrew verb tenses in
verse 6. It would be translated literally as: 'This poor man cried out' (past
perfect) 'and the LORD *was listening*' (past continuous).

This little grammar lesson brings out a wonderful truth. God hears us
when we cry to him; indeed, he is awaiting our cries for help. God means
us to pray to him, to come to him with our needs. We may only call on him
from time to time when it suits us, or when we remember or are in real
trouble, but God is permanently listening. David makes the same point
later: 'The righteous cry out, and the LORD hears them; he delivers them
from all their troubles' (34:17).

When we face a problem to which we can see no solution, we may say,
'All we can do is pray' – as if prayer were the last resort when all else has
failed! The Bible frequently tells us that prayer is the *best* thing we can do,
not the *last* thing we turn to. This whole psalm is a testimony to the fact
that God hears all our prayers. He may not answer when and how we want
him to – as we saw back in chapter 41 – but that is part of learning to trust

that he is the LORD. He knows best and 'we know that in all things God works for the good of those who love him, who have been called according to his purpose' (Rom 8:28).

God answers: a testimony

- Psalm 34 itself is not a prayer: there is not a single line addressed to God. Rather, it flows from statements of faith to personal testimony, and then back to encouraging statements about the goodness and faithfulness of the LORD. The whole psalm is a testimony to the way God has answered his prayer and an encouragement to all of us who read it to pray.
- It begins with a commitment to praise and glorify the Lord: 'I will extol the LORD at all times; his praise will always be on my lips' (34:1).
- It includes statements of faith: 'Those who look to him are radiant; their faces are never covered with shame' (34:5);'The eyes of the LORD are on the righteous, and his ears are attentive to their cry' (34:15).

It tells of answers to prayer: 'I sought the LORD, and he answered me; he delivered me from all my fears' (34:4); 'The LORD is close to the broken-hearted and saves those who are crushed in spirit (34:18); 'The righteous person may have many troubles, but the LORD delivers him from them all' (34:19).

As these last verses remind us, we are not immune from trouble. The writer reflects on his experience, and perhaps those of others he knew, and sees fears, troubles, broken hearts and people who are 'crushed in spirit'. The psalmist was realistic, but ultimately assuring. So too was Jesus, who said: 'In this world you will have trouble. But take heart! I have overcome the world' (Jn 16:33).

Encouragement to pray

David is very keen to encourage all who will listen to seek God and experience for themselves the goodness of God: 'Taste and see that the LORD is good; blessed is the one who takes refuge in him' (34:8); 'The lions may grow weak and hungry but those who seek the LORD lack no good thing' (34:10).

David is not claiming that God answers his prayers because he is someone special. No. Rather, he calls us to join him in honouring God: 'Glorify the LORD with me, let us exalt his name together' (34:4).

153

We are invited to taste and see that God is good, to trust him and prove for ourselves that he will help us and save us despite all our failings. 'The LORD will rescue his servants; no one who takes refuge in him will be condemned' (34:22).

Reflection

1. Read Psalm 34: What encouragement to pray do you find in this psalm?
2. What is your 'testimony' about how God has helped you in the past and answered prayer?
3. Take a few minutes to thank God for answers to your prayers in the past and bring your needs to God in prayer right now.

THE LIFE OF FAITH

Trusting God is a way of life in Psalms. It is the radical alternative to living on our wits or relying on our own wisdom, education, training, 'street smarts' and emotional intelligence.

To live by faith means 'confidence about what we hope for and assurance about what we do not see' (Heb 11:1). That is, we trust that God is there because he has revealed himself to us in creation, in his word and in Jesus Christ; and we trust that heaven is a reality because God has said in his word that it is and because Jesus rose again after death.

Psalms encourages us to put that faith into practice when life is difficult: when we are afraid (Ps 56:3–4); when we are doubting (143:8); when worries about the future crowd into our minds (37:5); when we find ourselves struggling spiritually (62:8); when we face opposition (25:1–2); and when it appears as though evil is winning (37:1–2). We are called to trust in God rather than rely on rich and powerful leaders (118:9) or our own resources (20:7).

God seems to have a way of building into our lives opportunities to exercise faith – not just an intellectual belief, or holding to a world view, but a personal trust in God – and to prove for ourselves that he is there and that his word is true. The following chapters look at some practical outcomes of living by faith: establishing priorities, taking a stand, recovering from failure, looking forward with hope, sleeping peacefully at night and finishing well.

47. ESTABLISHING PRIORITIES

Read Psalm 84

I would rather be a doorkeeper in the house of my God than dwell
in the tents of the wicked (84:10).

I cannot read this verse without thinking of my late father-in-law, who was a 'sidesman' in his local church. For him, the task of welcoming people to the church at the door and guiding them to their seats was a job he enjoyed. It was a job he performed with great commitment and care and one to which he was perfectly suited. He greeted people with genuine warmth and respect, mixed with a lovely sense of humour. He was a loving, caring man and his memory will remain with me as long as I live. He was happy to serve in this support role, rather than always hanker after more of the limelight.

This 'doorkeeper' had his priorities right.

First things first

The writer of Psalm 84 longed to be in the presence of God, with the people of God, above all else: 'My soul yearns, even faints, for the courts of the LORD; my heart and my flesh cry out for the presence of the living God' (84:2).

He makes clear his priorities with two key statements: firstly, a conviction about quality versus quantity in spending his precious, God-given time: 'Better is one day in your courts than a thousand elsewhere' (84:10). His mind may have ranged over all the demands on his time and the level of satisfaction he got from his life and concluded that one day in the presence of God was better than a thousand working, playing and relaxing without giving God a thought.

Secondly, the psalmist has a conviction about the true value of the 'important positions' we often strive for: 'I would rather be a doorkeeper in the house of my God than dwell in the tents of the wicked' (84:10). Here he states his priorities about work. He would rather have a lowly position and work with integrity, and in right relationship with God, than take a top job if that would compromise his values. He expresses his conviction that he won't 'miss out' by putting God first because God is no-one's debtor: 'The LORD bestows favour and honour' (84:11).

The best man at my wedding died of colon cancer at the age of 39. He was a highly successful Oxford University graduate who had joined the marketing department of a major international food company. He was upwardly mobile and destined for success in the corporate world.

My friend had no Christian background, but he came to faith in Christ in his early twenties, which had led him to reassess his priorities. He had gradually realised that he couldn't get passionate about the corporate ambition. He later told me: 'As I sat in yet another meeting with sales figures about why our competitors were selling more chocolate than us, I realised I had to get out. There were other things I cared a lot more about.' He later became a very successful high-school teacher in a low socio-economic inner-city area. He really cared about the children and young people he taught. He had found his true calling, albeit at a much lower salary and with much lower status. When he made the decision to change jobs, he could not have known that his life would be cut short. But as he was dying, he had the great satisfaction of knowing that he had done the right thing.

This one thing

Establishing priorities is good. Working out what we really value when 'the chips are down' is important. But best of all is settling once and for all that knowing God and serving him is our first priority: the one thing above all else that we value. Søren Kierkegaard, the nineteenth-century Danish Christian existential thinker, wrote a book entitled *Purity of Heart Is to Will One Thing*. The 'one thing' is what Kierkegaard described as 'the good'; he argued that 'the good' is a unity, and to pursue any other thing leads to double-mindedness. For most of us, the psalms make easier reading than Kierkegaard, but one truth is common to both: we all need to establish the single most important priority in our lives and to learn to value and pursue only what is eternally worthwhile.

Jesus frequently challenges our priorities directly and pointedly. Sometimes he does this with a rhetorical question: 'What good is it for someone to gain the whole world, yet forfeit their soul?' (Mk 8:36). Sometimes he does this with a command: 'Seek first his (God's) kingdom and his righteousness, and all these things will be given to you as well (Mt 6:33).

The Apostle Paul had clearly sorted out his top priority when he wrote these words: 'One thing I do: forgetting what is behind and straining toward what is ahead, I press on toward the goal to win the prize for which God has called me heavenward in Christ Jesus' (Phil 3:13–14).

Our priorities are revealed in our characters; what is truly important to us is shown in the way we spend our time and money. Our priorities also shape who we are, as we have seen in Proverbs.

You might like to make this your prayer: 'Lord please help me to set priorities in my life according to your word ... and help me to stick to them.'

'One thing I ask from the LORD, this only do I seek: that I may dwell in the house of the LORD all the days of my life' (27:4).

Reflection

1. What are the priorities in your life right now ... honestly?
2. What would it mean for you to put God first in your life?
3. Take a moment to assess your priorities in the light of Psalm 84 and Jesus' words above.

48. TAKING A STAND

Read Psalm 73

But as for me, it is good to be near God. I have made the Sovereign
LORD my refuge; I will tell of all your deeds (73:28).

We don't have many Bible texts scattered around our home, but one framed
card has accompanied us on all our travels over many years. It contains the
words of Joshua, spoken to the assembled people of Israel who were about
to disperse to their allotted areas after their arrival in the promised land.
Joshua warned them about all the temptations they would face to make
choices that would lead them away from God. He took his stand in front of
all the people with these words: 'But as for me and my household, we will
serve the LORD' (Josh 24:15).

That public commitment of Joshua, made so long ago, serves as a daily
reminder to me about where I stand in response to the grace of God.

Sometimes we feel as though we are alone – at work, in our communities
or even at home – in our convictions on matters of faith, integrity or fair
dealing. As we increasingly face questioning and scorn about matters of
faith, and outright opposition to Christianity, in Western countries, we
may feel unsure about how and when to make a stand. Indeed, we may be
wrestling with so many questions that we are unsure what we really believe
anymore. Past certainties may no longer be so clear-cut. Taking a stand can
be a lonely business.

Stopping the slide

The writer of Psalm 73 was on a slippery slope. He was grappling with
the question of why evil people seem to prosper in defiance of God. As he
struggled with the implications of this observation, he felt that his faith
was failing: 'But as for me, my feet had almost slipped; I had nearly lost
my foothold. For I envied the arrogant when I saw the prosperity of the
wicked' (73:2–3).

As he looked around, he saw people who appeared to be successful
and free from care. They seemed to have dispensed with religion and they
mocked the existence of God, yet they experienced no ill effect (73:4–11).
Indeed, they appeared to experience the opposite: 'always free of care, they
go on amassing wealth' (73:12).

Reflecting on this, he starts to come to the conclusion that his faith and religious practice have all been a waste of time. But, in order to avoid dragging others down with him, he does not want to express these doubts aloud (73:15). Was all that he had believed and stood for in his life really 'in vain'?

In mountain climbing, if you are sliding down a dangerous cliff face, the most important thing is to stop the slide. If you are on a steep snow or ice face, you need to apply the ice axe in a braking position. Nothing else matters at that point. So it is with our faith: when we are losing our hold spiritually, we need to stop the slide. How does the psalmist do it?

In verse 17, the whole tenor of the psalm changes. The writer goes – perhaps more out of duty than desire – to worship God. In that experience, God reminds him of eternity and of the future destruction of all these seemingly successful people (73:19). While praying and worshipping God, he remembers the presence of God and the promises of God: 'Yet I am always with you; you hold me by my right hand. You guide me with your counsel, and afterwards you will take me into glory. Whom have I in heaven but you? And earth has nothing I desire besides you' (73:24–25).

His mind is cleared and he gets things back in proportion. He realises that nothing matters more than knowing God. He reaffirms his faith in these words: 'My flesh and my heart may fail, but God is the strength of my heart and my portion forever' (73:26).

The psalmist concludes by letting us know exactly where he stands as he faces the future, whatever those around him may say or do. 'But as for me, it is good to be near God. I have made the Sovereign LORD my refuge; I will tell of all your deeds' (73:28).

As for me …

Friendship, family and Christian fellowship are some of God's great gifts to us. But we can't hide in the crowd when facing life's big questions. Reading the Gospels, it is striking how many times we find Jesus dealing one-to-one with people. Think, for example, of Nicodemus, of the woman at the well, the man born blind and Peter on the lake shore. Jesus calls us to a personal relationship. He calls each of us to make our stand for him, to be unafraid and unashamed to identify with him (Mk 8:38).

This need to take a stand is nothing new. The prophet Micah, in the eight century BC, looked at the disintegrating community around him, where 'the faithful have been swept from the land' (7:2). The society of his day was characterised by corruption, violence, deceit and the breakdown of family life (7:3–6). (Does that sound familiar?) He decided it was time to make his stand: 'But as for me, I watch in hope for the LORD; I wait for God my Saviour; my God will hear me' (Mic 7:7).

Whether in the face of external opposition or internal doubts and fears, there come times when we need to say to ourselves and to others 'As for me …' In the words of another psalm: 'As for me, I shall always have hope; I will praise you more and more' (71:14).

Reflection

1. 'As for me …': where and how have you made a stand for what you believe?

2. Is there an issue where you need to make a clear stand right now, in a matter of faith, principle or behaviour?

   For example, on what you watch on TV and internet sites?

   > I will not look with approval on anything that is vile. I hate what faithless people do; I will have no part in it. The perverse of heart shall be far from me; I will have nothing to do with what is evil (101:3–4).

   Or, in a commitment to honour God?

   > As for me, I will declare this forever; I will sing praise to the God of Jacob who says, 'I will cut off the horns of all the wicked, but the horns of the righteous will be lifted up' (75:9).

   Or, in a commitment to stick close to God and testify to what he has done?

   > 'But as for me, it is good to be near God. I have made the Sovereign LORD my refuge; I will tell of all your deeds (73:28).

3. Read Psalm 101 as a statement of personal resolve.

49. RECOVERING FROM FAILURE

Read Psalm 78

But he brought his people out like a flock; he led them like sheep
through the wilderness. … But they put God to the test and
rebelled against the Most High (78:52, 56).

Our failures don't take God by surprise. All of us may fail to achieve what
we want to achieve or to be the people we want to be. We certainly all fail
to be the people God wants us to be.

I find it encouraging that the Bible is full of examples of human failure.
Adam failed to obey the simplest instruction. Cain failed to love his brother.
Abraham failed the honesty test. Gideon and Sampson, and even the great
prophet Elijah, failed to trust God consistently. David failed morally, Peter
failed Jesus in his time of greatest need – and so it goes on. The Bible does
not airbrush its portraits of men and women of faith. They are shown as
fallible people, but still loved by God.

The failure of God's people

Psalm 78 looks back over the history of God's people as a whole, rather
than focusing on individuals, but the view is similar. The psalmist sees a
recurring pattern of failure.

The failure of God's people highlighted here is threefold: they didn't
keep God's covenant, they refused to live by his law and they forgot the
wonderful things he had done for them (78:9– 10). The people of Israel,
who had seen God rescue them from slavery in Egypt and lead them across
the Red Sea and through the desert, continued to sin against him.

'They wilfully put God to the test by demanding the food they craved.
They spoke against God; they said, "Can God really spread a table in the
wilderness?"' (78:18–19).

God had indeed spread a table for them. He had given them a daily
supply of food, brought them meat and shown them in supernatural ways
that he was providing for them. And yet, 'in spite of all this, they kept on
sinning; in spite of his wonders they did not believe' (78:32).

The result? One of the saddest comments in all Scripture: '[God] ended
their days in futility' (78:33). The Israelites were destined to wander around
the desert, going nowhere. Apart from Joshua and Caleb, they did not get
to see the promised land. From time to time, they did turn back to God,

not because they loved him but because it looked like a smart thing to do to stay alive (78:34–36). But God was not fooled. He knew 'their hearts were not loyal to him, they were not faithful to his covenant' (78:37).

As the writer looks back to all the miraculous signs God gave them when he delivered them from slavery in Egypt, and then how he brought them through the desert to the promised land, he notes, sadly, 'They put God to the test and rebelled against the Most High' (78:56).

This psalm must have been written in the early years of David's kingship, because it concludes on a note of celebration that God has sent them David as a deliverer and wise ruler (78:65–72). If it had been written later, it might well have gone on to record the failures of David, which are many and are faithfully recorded in Scripture (see, for example, 1 Samuel 11 and 12).

Learning from failure

If we go back to the first eight verses of the psalm, we are told *why* the writer wanted to focus on this sad picture of failure. It wasn't to wallow in a pit of negativity; it was so that future generations would learn from these mistakes and not be like their forebears, 'a stubborn and rebellious generation, whose hearts were not loyal to God' (78:8).

God wants us to learn from him, our own failures and the failures of others, particularly those of the people of Israel long ago. Two New Testament letters make this clear: 'Now these things occurred as examples to keep us from setting our hearts on evil things as they did' (1 Cor 10:6); and, 'See to it, brothers and sisters, that none of you has a sinful, unbelieving heart that turn away from the living God' (Heb 3:12).

We are to learn from Israel's mistakes. It sounds simple, but the problem is that we are made of the same stuff. We quickly forget God's goodness to us. We quickly default to self-reliance and say to ourselves, 'I am the master of my fate, I am the captain of my soul.'[55]

Rather than trusting and obeying our God, we want to put our own stamp of authority on our lives. In the words of the prophet Isaiah, 'We all, like sheep, have gone astray' (Isa 53:6).

So what's the good news?

God's patience with us

Let's read this psalm again, but this time looking at the character and works of God rather than at the failure of the people. The failures are well documented, but let's not miss the bigger, more important theme of the patient grace of God.

---

55 From 'Invictus' by William Ernest Henry (1849–1903).

Look what God did for the Israelites despite their failure and rebellion. He delivered them from their enemies. He showed them his great power. He provided for them when they were hungry.

Most wonderful of all, 'he was merciful; he forgave their iniquities and did not destroy them. Time after time he restrained his anger and did not stir up his full wrath. He remembered that they were but flesh' (78:38–39).

It was not through any self-help program that the people of Israel turned their failures back into success. It was because God graciously forgave them and renewed them.

This is the message that we can take from Psalm 78. God knows us and knows we are more than likely to fail, just as his people have done since the beginning of human life. But, whatever our failures – whatever we have done and however long we have neglected him – as we turn to him, he will again 'shine his face' upon us and forgive us, enabling us go forward with him.

God is faithful to his covenant promises even when we fail.

Reflection

1. What lessons have you learned from 'failures' in your own life? How have you recovered from those failures? What have you learned from God in the process?
2. Read Psalm 78 and list all the ways in which the people failed. Which ones resonate with you? Then list all the ways in which God shows his patience and grace.

50. LOOKING FORWARD WITH HOPE

Read Psalm 16

You will not abandon me to the realm of the dead, nor will you
let your faithful one see decay. You have made known to me the
path of life; you will fill me with joy in your presence, with eternal
pleasures at your right hand (16:10–11).

Psalm 16 is something of a 'breathing space', a moment in time when David,
the author, reflects on the good things of life and thanks God for them.

'LORD, you alone are my portion and my cup; you make my lot secure.
The boundary lines have fallen for me in pleasant places; surely I have a
delightful inheritance' (16:5–6).

This psalm is a declaration of faith, and it is full of confident hope. It
begins with a prayer to God for safety (16:1) and then makes a statement of
commitment and devotion to Yahweh (LORD) as Lord (16:2–5). David goes
on to remind himself of the blessings of being in that covenant relationship
(16:7–9). The psalm ends on a note of assurance: that his relationship with
God will go on beyond the grave (16:10–11).

Hope in eternal life

Many psalms point clearly to life after death as the continuation of
a relationship with the LORD begun on earth. The psalmists seem to
have a firm (if not fully developed) grasp of the 'now' and the 'not yet':
the enjoyment of God's presence in this life and the promise of perfect
fulfilment in the next (see, for example, 11:7; 49; 73:24).

The author of Psalm 49 declares: 'God will redeem me from the realm
of the dead; he will surely take me to himself' (49:15). And here, in Psalm
16: 'You will not abandon me to the realm of the dead … you will fill me
with joy in your presence' (16:10, 11).

This understanding of eternal life is developed much further in the New
Testament, where the resurrection of Jesus is described as the 'firstfruits' of
the resurrection of all believers (1 Cor 15:20).

The Apostle Peter must have learned Psalm 16 growing up, but perhaps
he learned its deeper meaning from Jesus. He quotes this psalm at length
in his speech to the crowd in Jerusalem on the day of Pentecost (Acts 2:25–
28). The Apostle Paul similarly refers to this psalm when pointing to the
resurrection of Jesus (Acts 13:35).

I find it very sad when I talk to non-believing retirees who have no hope for the future and realise that their best years are now behind them. For the Christian, the opposite is true. To be with Christ is 'far better' (Phil 1:23).

Hope for the coming Messiah

The use of Psalm 16 in the New Testament shows it to be a messianic psalm, one that pointed towards the coming Messiah, the Christ.[56] The psalmists, who lived in days when even the best earthly leaders failed to live up to their calling, looked forward in hope to the coming of God's promised king who would bring justice and peace.

Many of the psalms point in different ways towards the coming of Jesus, the Christ. We have psalms that speak of the Sonship of the Messiah (2:7), his divinity (110), his suffering (22:1; 31:5), his reforming zeal (69:9), his isolation (69:7–12), his deliberate self-offering (40:6–8), the manner of his death (22:16) and his being betrayed, hated and rejected (41:9, 69:4, 35:19). He was 'the stone the builders rejected' (118:22) who would become the capstone, or cornerstone, of God's temple.

We look forward to the second coming of Jesus, promised by Jesus himself (Jn 14:3) and proclaimed by the apostles (1 Thess 4:13–18; 2 Pet 3:3–13). The certainty of his coming is to be a source of joy and encouragement to us, and an inspiration to live a godly life along the way (Titus 2:11–13) – just as the hope of his first coming was to the psalmists.

Hope in the present

The psalmist's statement, 'You make known to me the path of life' (16:11), seems to have a double meaning. God shows us the path *to* life: eternal life, dwelling with him forever. He also sets a path for us to follow here on earth, a path *of* life: a life travelled with God, relying on his guidance and teaching, and enjoying his constant presence, which allows us to face any opposition and overcome any situation.

We find a wonderful statement in Proverbs that seems to have a similar double meaning: 'The path of the righteous is like the morning sun, shining ever brighter till the full light of day' (Prov 4:18). It is a picture of having our backs to the darkness as we walk *towards* the light and as we walk *in* the light (1 Jn 1:7). This is surely how God want us to live: looking with confidence to the fulfilment of his promises, the coming again of Jesus

---

56 The Hebrew (Old Testament) word 'Messiah' means 'anointed'; that is, anointed to be king. 'Christ' is the Greek (New Testament) term for 'anointed one'.

Christ to wind up human history; and, in the meantime, living each day sure in the hope that God is at work in his world and in our lives.

'I keep my eyes always on the LORD. With him at my right hand I will not be shaken' (Ps 16:8).

Reflection

1. How much does the prospect of seeing the Lord's return, and being with him forever, affect the way you live now?
2. What practical steps can you take to keep this wonderful prospect 'front of mind' each day?
3. Read 2 Peter 3:3–15. In the light of the Lord's promised return, how should we then live?

51. SLEEPING PEACEFULLY AT NIGHT

Read Psalms 3, 4, and 6

In peace I will lie down and sleep, for you alone, LORD, make me
dwell in safety (4:8).

Sleep, they say, is a great healer. It is certainly a great blessing. The more
trouble we have sleeping, the more we learn to value a good night's sleep.

Troubled nights

'I am worn out from my groaning. All night long I flood my bed with
weeping and drench my couch with tears' (6:6).

The writer of Psalm 6 was in a seriously bad way. He could not sleep; he
was exhausted with grief, and cried out to God for relief: 'Heal me, LORD,
for my bones are in agony. My soul is deep in anguish' (6:2–3).

A friend of ours suffers from chronic back pain and is unable to sleep
without painkillers and, occasionally, sleeping pills. She can certainly relate
to these words.

There are many reasons why we may not sleep well at night. Parents
with newborns or sick children may be sleep-deprived for months. Noise
from a neighbour's party or traffic noise from a nearby busy road may keep
us awake for hours. Our body clocks may be out of sync due to shift work or
jetlag. Body pains and aches always make sleep difficult, or we may simply
have been drinking too much caffeine or alcohol or eating too much rich
food. We lie awake in some discomfort, regretting our over-indulgence. I
lived in a tent in an African game reserve for over a year when I was in my
twenties. I sometimes found sleep difficult, particularly when I heard the
lions grunting and occasionally roaring nearby, or when hyenas came into
my kitchen tent and started trying to eat my bowls and pans!

Most of us know what it is like to lie awake in the dark, tossing and
turning with anxious thoughts racing through our minds. Worries can
keep us awake, sometimes for hours, as we turn problems over and over in
our minds. We can't stop worries flooding into our minds, but we can turn
them into prayer and even praise.

The psalms help us turn sleeplessness into something good: 'I will
praise the LORD, who counsels me; even at night my heart instructs me'
(16:7); 'On my bed I remember you; I think of you through the watches of
the night' (63:6).

We can use sleepless hours to meditate on God's word, listening to worship songs or Bible talks. If our worries are due to our own sin and guilt, then we may need to get out of bed, get on our knees, confess our sin and receive God's forgiveness (1 Jn 1:9).

Faith or fear?

One of the most common reasons for sleeplessness is fear. You may know that awful fear of waking up in pain in the middle of the night, unable to get back to sleep, wondering whether you should call a doctor. We may fear burglars and attack, fear for the safety of our children and grandchildren, or be troubled by fears we can't quite put a name to.

David, the author of Psalm 3, was in big trouble. He was on the run from his own son Absalom, who had usurped David's throne and was out to kill him. David describes his life in danger, being surrounded by enemies and mocked by people who regarded him as out of favour with God (3:2). He had good reason to lie awake at night worrying.

And yet, David is able to say: 'I lie down and sleep; I wake again, because the LORD sustains me. I will not fear though tens of thousands assail me on every side' (3:5–6).

Though under duress, David turns to the LORD as his shield (protector) and the one who 'lifts up his head'. Body language is clear here. When we are dispirited, our heads go down. Look at a file of refugees leaving their homeland, or even a losing football team: their heads are down. But God is the one who lifts up our heads. Why? Because he answers prayer for help: 'I call out to the LORD, and he answers me from his holy mountain' (3:4).

David affirms that he can sleep peacefully at night, free from fear. He doesn't fear, because the LORD is his protector and deliverer. He will wake up in the morning knowing that the LORD has looked after him and strengthened him (3:5).

Day or night, God does not intend us to live in fear.

An evening meditation

In Psalm 4, David is again in distress (4:1). His leadership and authority have again been challenged, and his enemies have made false promises to the people (4:2).

This psalm seems to have been written in the evening. As Kidner comments, 'The approach of night, with its temptation to brood on past wrongs and present perils, only challenges David to make his faith explicit and to urge it on others as a committal of one's cause and oneself to a faithful Creator.'[57]

In this unsettling situation, David 'centres' himself on the LORD his God, like a magnetic compass turning to true north after being shaken about. Even in great distress, David finds joy in his spiritual relationship with the LORD, which is greater than any joy that material blessings can bring (4:7). It is in this context, and in this confidence, that David asserts, 'In peace I will lie down and sleep, for you alone, LORD make me dwell in safety' (4:8).

Whatever our health problems, worries or fears, whatever our sleep patterns, Psalms reminds us that security and peace is to be found in trusting God.

Reflection

1. Read Proverbs 3:21–26. What reasons are given for being able to sleep without fear?
2. What encouragement do we find in the Bible to deal with worry? See, for example, Matthew 6:25–34 and Philippians 4:6.

   You may like to use this old prayer at the end of each day:

   > Lighten our darkness, we beseech thee, O Lord; and by thy great mercy defend us from all perils and dangers of this night; for the love of thy only Son, our Saviour Jesus Christ. Amen.[58]

---

57 Kidner, *Psalms*, vol. 1, p. 55.
58 The Third Collect of Evening Prayer, *Book of Common Prayer*, 1662.

52. FINISHING WELL

Read Psalms 90 and 92

Our days may come to seventy years, or eighty if our strength
endures; yet the best of them are but trouble and sorrow, for they
quickly pass and we fly away (90:10).

It is one thing to prepare for death (as we considered in chapter 31); it is another to cope with the difficulties and constraints of old age.

Billy Graham wrote this at the age of 92: 'I never thought I would live to be this old. All my life I was taught how to die as a Christian, but no one ever taught me how I ought to live in the years before I die. I wish they had because I am an old man now, and believe me, it's not easy.'[59]

When we do pause to think about our own mortality, most of us hope that we die quietly in our sleep, surrounded by those we love, or, for the more adventurous, that we die while doing something we love to do. Of course, we have little control over how, when and where we die. When we see others being ravaged by cancer, multiple sclerosis or Alzheimer's, or hear of people we know experiencing a violent death, we can only pray and entrust ourselves to God.

Some things, though, we can control: not just our diets and exercise habits, but our *attitudes* to old age and the way we choose to use our diminishing physical and mental faculties. Most of all, we need to recognise that our time on earth is finite and ask God to help us to spend wisely the time he has given us: 'Teach us to number our days, that we may gain a heart of wisdom' (90:12).

Three things we might aim for as our life draws to a close: to be fruitful, a blessing to others right to the end; to pass on the truth of God to the next generation in whatever way we can; to keep trusting God in all things, big and small. Let us look at these together.

Being fruitful

What does it actually mean to be fruitful? This is not something we can do by ourselves. God's Spirit works in our lives to produce the fruit of a godly character: 'love, joy, peace, patience, kindness, goodness, faithfulness, gentleness, self-control' (Gal 5:22). It means that our lives will bless others.

---

59 Graham, *Nearing Home*, p vii.

The fruit that we grow on trees does not last. We pick it and eat it, or it falls to the ground and rots, or it is eaten by birds or other wildlife. By contrast, Jesus promised that fruit he produces in our lives will last. He promised: 'You did not choose me but I chose you and appointed you to go and bear fruit ... fruit that will last' (Jn 15:16).

The psalmist reminds us that God's purpose for our lives us is to grow strong in him and produce 'fruit', even when we are old!

> The righteous will flourish like a palm tree, they will grow like a cedar of Lebanon; planted in the house of the LORD, they will flourish in the courts of our God. They will still bear fruit in old age, they will stay fresh and green, proclaiming, 'the LORD is upright; he is my Rock, and there is no wickedness in him' (92:12–15).

The inscription that my late father chose to put on my mother's gravestone was: 'She was young at heart.' That was the way he wanted to remember her, even at eighty-two years of age, enjoying her life and brightening the lives of all those who knew her. As in the picture painted by the psalmist, she was bearing fruit in old age, 'fresh and green' right to the end.

Living with purpose

Wilf Green was of the finest Christians I have ever met. He had spent his life serving as a missionary in rural areas of Malawi and southern Africa. At the age of 65, when he could have started to enjoy retirement, he took on what became one of the most difficult challenges of his life, leading a church in a small town in Mauritius. Right to the end of his life, he was looking to help and serve others. Like the Apostle Paul, he lived purposefully and aimed to 'finish his course with joy' (Acts 20:24).

In Psalm 71, the psalmist prays that he will know God's presence and live purposefully to the end by passing on the truth about God to his children and grandchildren: 'Even when I am old and grey, do not forsake me, my God, till I declare your power to the next generation, your mighty acts to all who are to come' (71:18).

If you are in your later years, then you could ask God, 'What can I do for you – whether by writing, mentoring, teaching, encouraging or praying for the children and young people I know, or even starting a new adventure of faith?'

Living by faith

Finally, we will finish well if we continue to live by faith.

The writer of Psalm 78 notes that a whole generation of unbelieving people 'ended their years in futility' (78:33). They wouldn't trust God or listen to his word. By contrast, Abraham was still living by faith when he died (Heb 11:13). He was still looking forward in hope to what God had in store for him and doing the things God had for him to do.

So, let us press on and encourage one another to 'run the race set before us' (Heb 12:1). Then we can say with Paul at the end:

I have fought the good fight, I have finished the race, I have kept the faith. Now there is in store for me the crown of righteousness, which the Lord, the righteous Judge, will award to me on that day – and not only to me, but also to all who have longed for his appearing (2 Tim 4:7–8).

Reflection

1. Whatever your age or stage of life, what challenge and encouragement do you find in this psalm?
2. Think about the two images of trees presented in Psalm 92: the cedar of Lebanon and the palm tree (92:12–15). What truth is the psalmist trying to convey about God's purpose for your life?

Here is a simple prayer to pray:

Lord, please work in my life by your Spirit that I may live purposefully, fruitfully and faithfully right to the end.

BIBLIOGRAPHY

Proverbs

Kidner, Derek. *Proverbs: An Introduction and Commentary.* Tyndale Old Testament Commentaries. London: Inter-Varsity Press, 1964.

Moss, Alan. *Proverbs.* Sheffield: Sheffield Phoenix, 2015.

Waltke, Bruce K. *The Book of Proverbs.* 2 vols. Grand Rapids: Eerdmans, 2004.

Psalms

Athanasius. *The letter of Athanasius, Our Holy Father, Archbishop of Alexandria, to Marcellinus on the Interpretation of the Psalms.*

Calvin, John. *A Commentary on the Psalms.* Ed. T.H.L. Parker. Edinburgh: James Clarke & Co., 1965.

Goldingay, John. *Psalms.* 3 vols. Baker Academic, 2006

_____. *Songs from a Strange Land.* London: Inter-Varsity Press, 1978.

Kidner, Derek. *Psalms.* 2 vols. Tyndale Old Testament Commentaries. London: Inter-Varsity Press, 1973.

Lewis, C.S. *Reflections on the Psalms.* London: Fontana, 1967.

Mowinckel, Sigmund. *The Psalms in Israel's Worship.* Translated by D. R. Ap-Thomas. Grand Rapids: Eerdmans, 2004.

Weiser, Artur. *The Psalms: A Commentary.* London: SCM, 1962.

Westermann, Claus. The Living Psalms. Translated by J. R. Porter. Edinburgh: T & T Clark, 1989.

General

Augustine. *Confessions.* Translated by Henry Chadwick. Oxford: Oxford University Press, 1991.

Autton, Norman. *Peace at the Last: Talks with the Dying.* London: SPCK, 1978.

Bratt, James D., ed. *Abraham Kuyper: A Centennial Reader.* Grand Rapids: Eerdmans, 1998.

Calvin, John. *Institutes of the Christian Religion.* 2 vols. Edited by John T. McNeill, translated by Ford Lewis Battles. Library of Christian Classics, Volume 20. London: SCM, 1959.

Elliot, Elisabeth. *God's Guidance: A Slow and Certain Light.* New York: Revell, 1997.

Graham, Billy. *Nearing Home,* Nashville: Nelson, 2011.

Hill, Alexander. *Just Business.* 2nd edition. Downers Grove, IL: InterVarsity Press, 2008.

Hooper, Graham. *Undivided: Closing the Faith–Life Gap.* Nottingham: Inter-Varsity Press, 2013.

Lewis, C.S. Lewis, *Mere Christianity.* London: Fontana, 1972.

Lloyd-Jones, D. Martyn. *Spiritual Depression: Its Causes and Cures.* London: Pickering & Inglis, 1965.

Philips, Jennifer. *Bringing Lucy Home.* Nashville, TN: CrossBooks, 2015.

Stott, John. *The Radical Disciple: Wholehearted Christian Living.* Nottingham: Inter-Varsity Press, 2010.

Ten Boom, Corrie, Elizabeth Sherrill and John L. Sherrill. *The Hiding Place.*1st Hendrickson edition. Peabody, MA:, Hendrickson, 2009.

Young, Robert, William Barron Stevenson and William Foxwell Albright. *Analytical Concordance to the Bible.* 22nd American edition. Grand Rapids: Eerdmans, 1970.

Lightning Source UK Ltd.
Milton Keynes UK
UKOW01f0010100817

307028UK00011B/390/P